SOVIET T-55
MAIN BATTLE TANK

SOVIET T-55

MAIN BATTLE TANK

James Kinnear and Stephen L. (Cookie) Sewell

OSPREY PUBLISHING
Bloomsbury Publishing Plc
PO Box 883, Oxford, OX1 9PL, UK
1385 Broadway, 5th Floor, New York, NY 10018, USA
E-mail: info@ospreypublishing.com
www.ospreypublishing.com

OSPREY is a trademark of Osprey Publishing Ltd

First published in Great Britain in 2019

A catalogue record for this book is available from the British Library.

ISBN: HB 978 1 4728 3855 1; eBook 978 1 4728 3856 8; ePDF 978 1 4728 3856 8; XML 978 1 4728 3854 4

19 20 21 22 23 24   10 9 8 7 6 5 4 3 2 1

Index by Zoe Ross
Originated by PDQ Digital Media Solutions, Bungay, UK
Printed in China through World Print Ltd

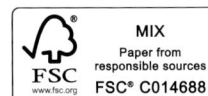

FSC
MIX
Paper from
responsible sources
FSC® C014688
www.fsc.org

Front cover: TOP: A T-55 M-1958 during Soviet Army manoeuvres. The glacis welding and lack of turret ventilator are distinguishing features of the T-55 as compared with the very similar T-54B. BOTTOM: Soviet T-55 M-1959 tanks advancing during manoeuvres. These tanks have a mix of wheel types, including the early T-44/T-54 'spiderweb' pattern wheel rarely seen on the T-55.
Back cover: UPPER: From many angles the T-55 is indistinguishable from the late production T-54B. The lack of turret roof ventilator is one major identifying feature. UPPER MIDDLE: A rare colour photograph of a Soviet Army T-55 with 'desant' riders, a wartime practice largely abandoned after tracked and wheeled APCs had entered service. LOWER MIDDLE: The T-55 was upgraded with explosive reactive armour as the T-55MV/AMV, with several fitment pattern types. BOTTOM: Several specialized combat vehicles were built on the T-55 chassis, including the IMR combat engineer vehicle.

PICTURE CREDITS
All pictures, including those on the cover, are from the author's collections unless otherwise noted. Artworks are by Andrey Aksenov and are credited where they appear.

NOTE ON THE TRANSLATION AND PRONUNCIATION OF RUSSIAN LANGUAGE
The Russian alphabet has more characters than the Latin-based English language, and the Russian language is also grammatically complex, and subject to varying translation depending on context, gender, time period and nationality of the translator. Therefore, it is not always possible to directly translate Russian terms or names into English, and the various means of doing so are contentious and often arbitrary. Translations of some Russian terms have also been simplified in this book without the contentious pronunciation accents, as although perceived correct by those with an academic but no practical experience of the language, use outside a dry academic environment makes the subsequent English translation of a living Russian language difficult to read. An example is Ob'iekt (object) that has been simplified as Obiekt for consistency with previously published books. As these books are technical histories rather than studies of Russian grammar, the authors trust that this simplification of translation and terminology makes the books easier to read than would be the case if all the contentious accents were included.

Osprey Publishing supports the Woodland Trust, the UK's leading woodland conservation charity.

To find out more about our authors and books visit **www.ospreypublishing.com**. Here you will find extracts, author interviews, details of forthcoming events and the option to sign up for our newsletter.

CONTENTS

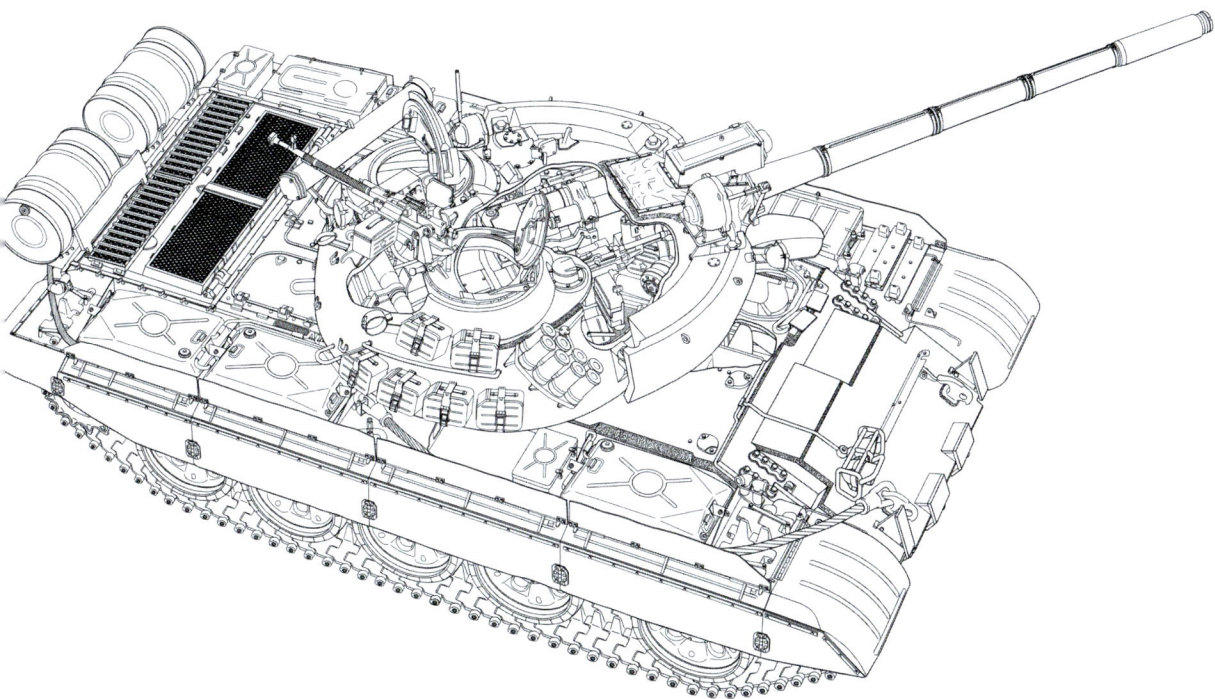

INTRODUCTION

While it was closely related to the previous T-44 and T-54 tank designs, the T-55 is one of the most iconic weapons created by the Soviet Union during the Cold War and also one of the most widely distributed major weapons in history. Approximately 23,000 T-55 tanks of all versions were produced by the Soviet Union beginning in 1958, with another approximately 15,000 built by Poland and Czechoslovakia, a small number of derivatives built in Romania and thousands of other related variants produced by the People's Republic of China.

The T-55 tank was essentially what the Russians refer to as a 'rationalized' version of the T-54B tank. A 'rationalizer' was the term used for someone who simplifies, improves, finds a better way to build, or cuts the cost of making any sort of item they produced. While the tank suffered from the emerging drawback of its direct forebear – monolithic homogeneous armour

A line-up of Soviet army T-55 tanks during manoeuvres. The T-55 was, from a distance, almost indistinguishable from the late T-54B, but small details such as the glacis plate welding identified the type.

– it was nevertheless simple to operate, easy to repair in the field, and relatively dependable if normal maintenance was ensured. When compared to its progenitor (the T-44), the T-55 encompassed a large number of relatively sophisticated and compact systems in a tank not much larger than the preceding T-44.

The T-55 tank evolved from the combination of previous work undertaken by Soviet designers including F. F. Petrov, who created its lightweight and powerful 100mm gun, and I. Ya. Trashutin, the designer of the V-2 series of diesel engines, combined with the concepts of Aleksandr Morozov already used in the proven T-54. But the man ultimately responsible for this tank was Leonid Nikolayevich Kartsev, then the chief designer at the Ural Railway Wagon Construction Plant (Ural'ny Vagonstroitel'sviy Zavod – UVZ). He believed in the evolutionary system of tank development, which ran counter to Aleksandr Morozov's thinking about revolutionary designs. In later years, after Kartsev was no longer responsible for its further development, the T-55 tank received massive upgrades with through-the-bore anti-tank missile capability, laser rangefinders, increased engine power output and new running gear, and, on differing models, either passive or active protective measures. These upgrades maintained the currency of the T-55 tank infinitely longer than its original planned Soviet service life.

This book is in large part based on existing research undertaken by Russian armour historians and veterans of the Soviet tank industry, and now available in the unclassified world. To this day Soviet and Russian post-World War II state archives are essentially barred to Western researchers, so the efforts of these individuals are greatly appreciated. Most of them will be identifiable from the bibliography used in the research for this book. As with any such work, the result is based on the collective efforts of many individuals who provided archive and photographic material, as well as correcting errors and omissions. Thanks in particular go to Andrey Aksenov, Yuri Pasholok, Sergei Popsuevich and Igor Zheltov. Credit must also be given to acknowledged experts in the field such as Steve Zaloga and Christopher Foss. They have provided both information and advice on approaching this subject.

A T-55AM modernized in Ukraine on display.

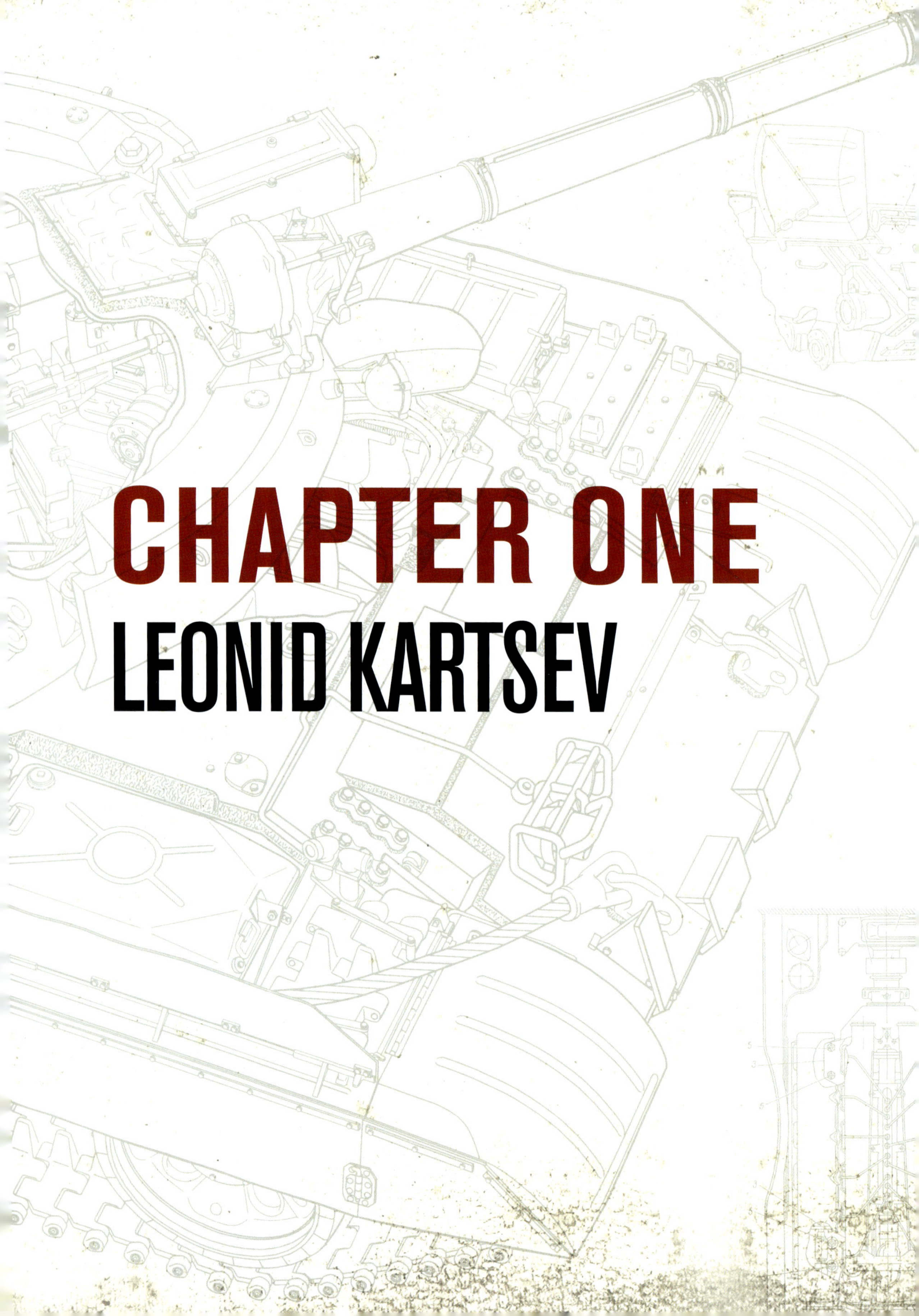

CHAPTER ONE
LEONID KARTSEV

A cross-section of the engine pre-heater system redesigned by Kartsev as his first assignment at the UVZ.

Leonid Nikolayevich Kartsev was the first chief designer of Soviet tanks to be born after the Russian Revolution, and the first one to grow up completely under the schooling and inculcation of the Communist Party. He progressed to become one of the premier Soviet tank designers, remaining in position for a period of almost three decades. During this time he would professionally rival two of the established giants of the industry – Aleksandr Morozov in Kharkov and Zhosef Kotin in Leningrad – and would develop three major post-war tank designs, namely the T-55, the T-62 and the T-72.

Born on 21 July 1922, in the small village of Skomovo Gavrilovo in the Posadsky region of Ivanovo Oblast (located between Yaroslavl and Nizhny Novgorod), like many others Kartsev was drafted into the Red Army at the age of 19. He served in the Great Patriotic War as a tank mechanic and after the war attended the Military Academy of the Armoured Forces from which he graduated in 1949, being thereafter posted to Plant No. 183 (Uralvagonzavod – UVZ) in Nizhny Tagil as an engineer.

Kartsev rose quickly through the design engineer ranks as he was clearly a talented engineer. In 1953, as many of the UVZ designers based in Nizhny Tagil were being returned to the Kharkov Steam Locomotive Factory (KhPZ – the Kharkov tank plant) where they had worked prior to the war, a decision had to be made as to who would be appointed as the new chief designer at the plant. Morozov was clearly aware that his favourite deputy and right-hand man, Yakov 'Yariy' Baranov, was the first choice, but he wanted Baranov to go back to

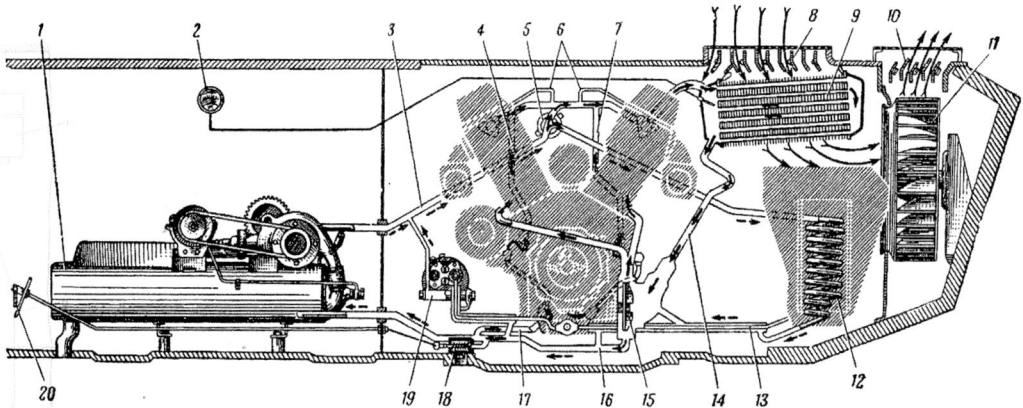

Kharkov with him to help re-establish the pre-war design bureau there, so he lobbied Moscow very heavily for such a result. The only other eligible candidate, Nikolai Kucherenko, had been selected to work at 'Glavtank' (Main Directorate for Tank Building of the Ministry of Transport Machine Building (MTrM) of the USSR) in Moscow. Once it was a fait accompli the new appointee was declared as Leonid Kartsev.

Kartsev's first task as chief design engineer at UVZ was to oversee the design and production of the later production models of the T-54 medium tank fitted with gun stabilizers – first the T-54A with a single-axis stabilizer, and subsequently the T-54B with a twin-axis stabilizer. But by 1953, so many individual changes had been made to the initial T-54 design that some 'rationalizing' improvements were necessary to streamline the alterations being made on the assembly line.

Kartsev took over full control of the complete upgrade and improvement of the T-54 tank, resulting in Obiekt (Object) 137G2. This tank featured many detail improvements to the T-54B design, making it more functional and easier to manufacture, and also made some operation design changes in the process. One of the first modifications came as a result of changing aircraft technology both in the Soviet Union and abroad. By the mid 1950s, propeller-driven ground attack aircraft such as the Soviet IL-2 'Shturmovik' and its foreign counterparts had been replaced by jet-engined aircraft, against which the turret-mounted 12.7mm DShKM

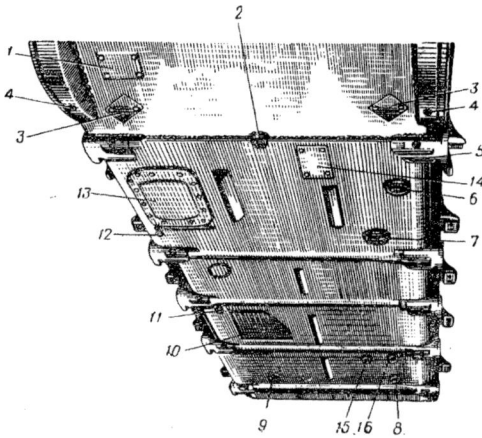

ABOVE The manual view of the hull floor of the T-55 tank, showing the new location of the escape hatch (lower left) and access panels for draining fluids from the engine.
BELOW A cross-section of the T-55 Model 1958 tank.

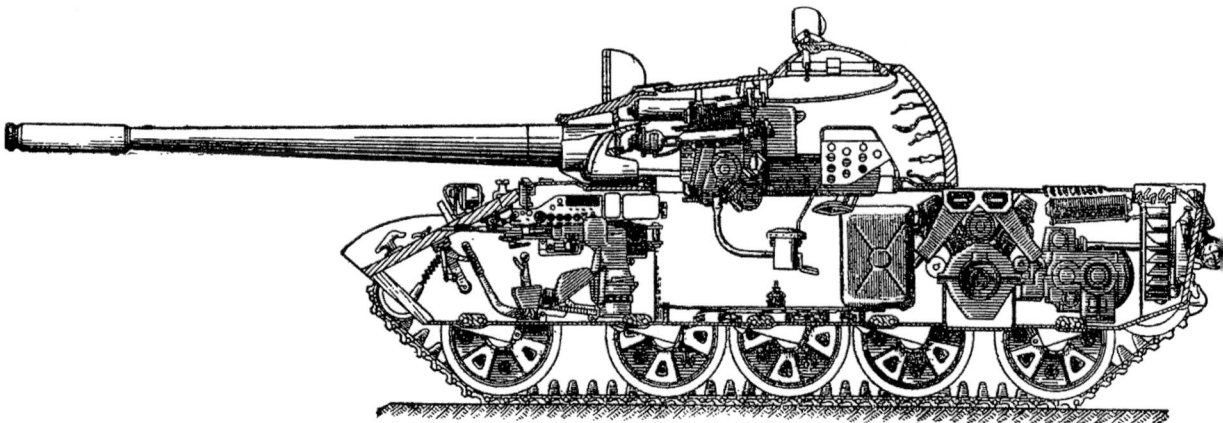

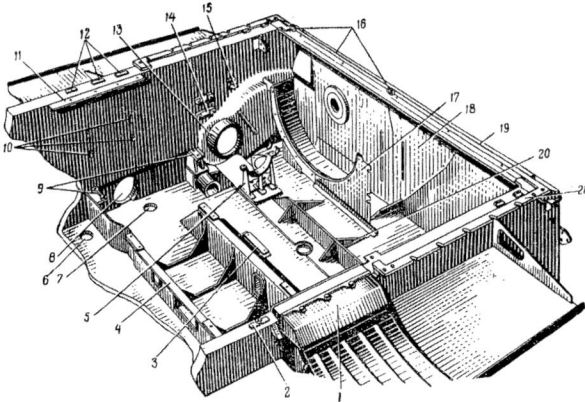

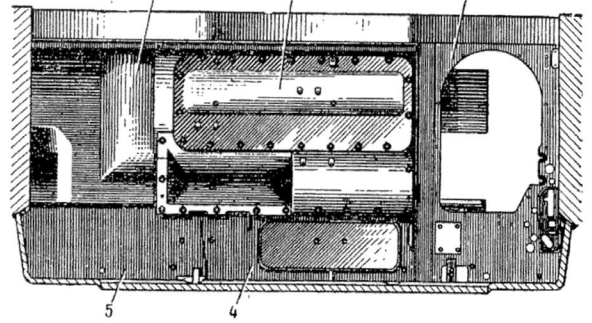

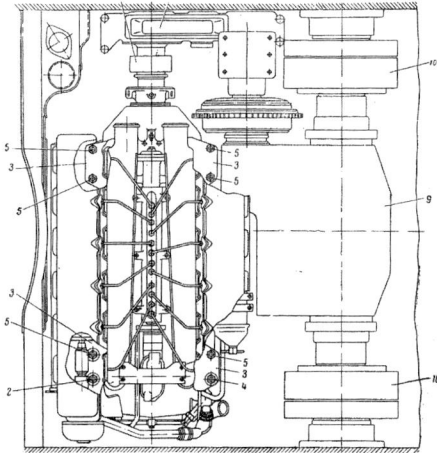

ABOVE LEFT The engine-transmission bay of the T-55 tank.
ABOVE RIGHT The firewall between the engine-transmission compartment and fighting compartment of the T-55 (left side is the right end).
LEFT Schematic of the power plant installation in the T-55 tank. Centre left at the top is the 'guitara' transfer case from the engine to the transmission which permitted the T-44, T-54 and T-55 tanks to be more compact than the earlier designs.
BELOW The fuel tank layout for all T-55 tanks prior to the M versions in the 1980s. This now includes the twin 'stellazh' ammo rack/fuel cells in the bow.

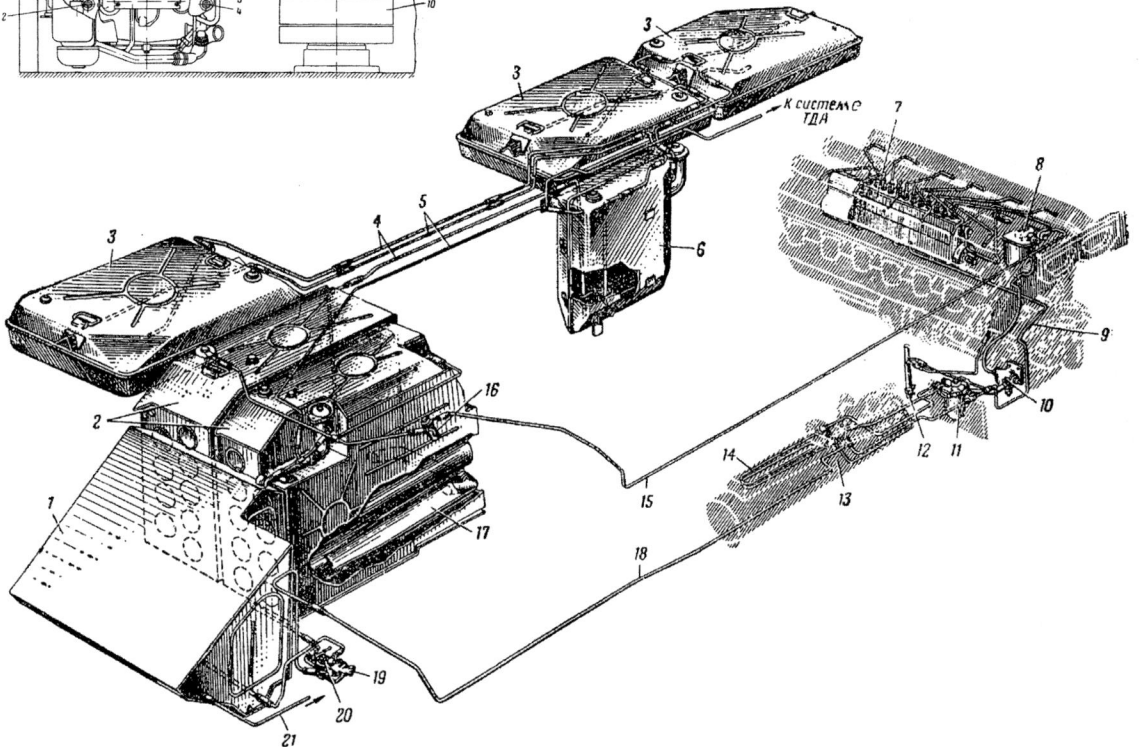

anti-aircraft machine gun was ineffective. In consequence, the heavy 12.7mm anti-aircraft machine gun mount used on the T-54 tanks was removed and replaced with a simple domed hatch. Eventually the new design, incorporating all the elements of the T-54B and new design features and upgrades in a modified package, was redesignated Obiekt-155 and given the service designator T-55 medium tank.

The Obiekt-140 was also considered as a potential replacement for the T-54, but was not accepted for series production. Elements of the future T-62 and T-72 are evident in this surviving prototype, located in the Kubinka 'scrapyard' in the early 1990s.

Series production of the T-55 tank began within Department 520 at UVZ in Nizhny Tagil in 1958. As production was only just beginning, the plant considered the developing Soviet doctrine of potential combat within a tactical nuclear warfare environment, and the design requirements for a tank capable of operating in such an environment. The plant developed a new variant of the tank that was capable, albeit for a limited time period, of surviving and operating on a nuclear battlefield. The result emerged in 1961 as the T-55A, fitted with a lead-impregnated plastic liner (*nadboy*) inside the occupied parts of the tank and external liners (*podboy*) over those parts of the tank that could not be fitted with liners, such as the access hatches for the crew and some parts of the turret.

NST – NEW MEDIUM TANK

While the above described was the operational activity being carried out for ongoing current production, at the time Kartsev took over the design bureau a requirement had also been handed down from Moscow for the Novy Sredny Tank (NST) or New Medium Tank. Initially Yariy Baranov had been in charge of the project before he departed back to Kharkov, and then it became Kartsev's project. In the summer of 1954 he presented his new design, Obiekt-140. This tank resembled an evolved T-54 with six smaller road wheels and new 'live' track design, a new engine, and armed with the long-barrelled 100mm D-54TS rifled gun. The Kharkov design, the Obiekt-430, was altogether more radical, using a new hull design, new turret design, lightweight running gear, and a radical experimental 4TD four-cylinder opposed piston two-stroke diesel engine, a significant move away from the staple V-12 diesel of known reliability used in Soviet tanks since the mid 1930s.

The Kharkov engine design was ultimately rejected, but Morozov instead pressed for the even more advanced 5TD five-cylinder design. Moscow fought Morozov's viewpoint as being a potential 'money pit', and asked him to locate another engine design for the new tank. One such engine offered to him was a shorter variant of the V-2 design from Barnaul called the 8D12U; he refused it, but Kartsev took it for the Obiekt-140. Both tank prototypes emerged in early 1957 (Obiekt-140 from UVZ and Obiekt-430 from Plant No. 75 in Kharkov), with both tanks undergoing a very protracted testing process that lasted into 1960.

In 1958, however, when the powers in Moscow were assessing the two tanks, Kartsev had nearly committed political and professional suicide when he stated before the technical committee that neither tank was going to offer a major advantage or improvement over the T-54 and T-55 tanks, and so should be cancelled. He pointed out that their armour was still monolithic cast steel; the designs were little changed over their predecessors; speed, mobility and range were only modestly improved; and if produced, they would be a waste of money and development effort. While his assessment was straightforward and technically entirely accurate, as a result he made many enemies in both the Scientific Advisory Council to the Politburo (Technical Council) and also among the Kharkov personnel, who were convinced they had a superior design. Failings in the Obiekt-430 would later force a complete redesign of the tank as the Obiekt-432, which eventually became the series production T-64 main battle tank.

After his forthrightness in 1958, Kartsev would thereafter have some political difficulties, being seen by some in authority as what is referred to today as 'not a team player', and as such his new designs were the subject of negative criticism that was often more political than technical. When Morozov's Obiekt-432 could not be made to run consistently, and with demands from people like Ground Forces Commander Marshal Chuikov for a larger-calibre tank gun being required in service with immediate effect, Kartsev modified the T-55 design to take a larger turret

Airflow pathway from air intake to engine and exhaust to outlet.

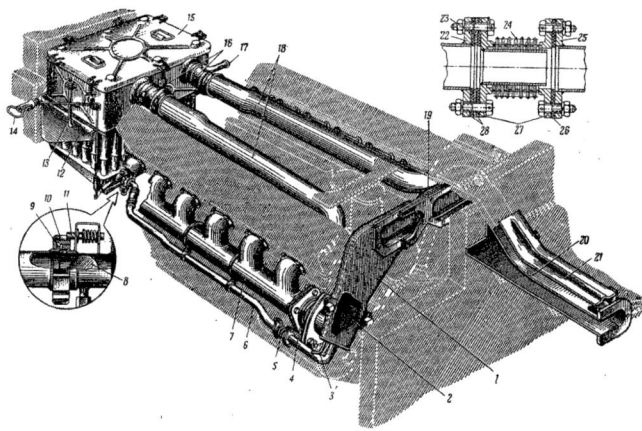

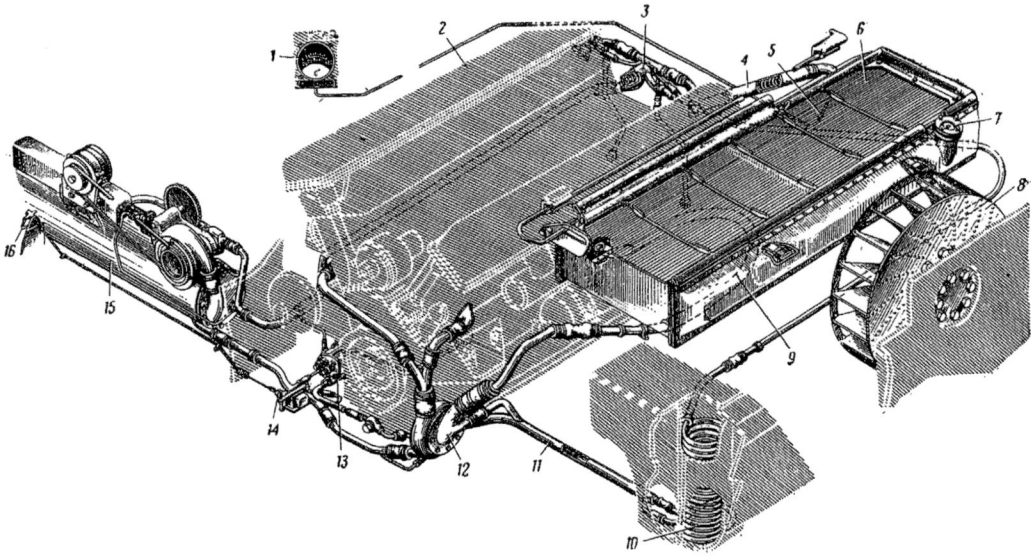

ABOVE Engine cooling system showing the pre-heater on the left and the flow of coolant through the engine and radiator.
BELOW Transmission component layout: 1 – 'guitara'; 2 – main clutch; 3 – gearbox; 4 – final drives; 5 – fan.

A T-55 M-1958 during driver-mechanic training. The tank is negotiating a wooden railway wagon off-ramp which may or may not be connected to lowbed railway wagons.

mounting the 115mm U-5TS smoothbore gun. But none of the Technical Council personnel would accept his new tank, even though it was clearly an incremental 'low risk' design with more powerful armament but based on the known reliability of the T-55 lineage. Minister of Defence Marshal of the Soviet Union Grechko solved the problem by designating the new tank as a 'tank destroyer' rather than a tank and ordering it into immediate production. Some 20,000 of these new tanks were eventually built as the T-62 medium tank.

T-55 Model 1958 tanks on exercise. The foreground tank (429) appears to have one of the early mounts for the two-section snorkel and also may be carrying a field stove (pipes on the right handrail and what appears to be the collapsed stove on the turret rear) for cooking in the field.

When Obiekt-432 was meanwhile being subjected to increased testing and showing increasing failures, Kartsev offered up another new tank based on the T-62 design but with new running gear fitted with return rollers and rubber-bushed RMSh tracks, which were anticipated to increase track life from 2,000 kilometres for the OMSh tracks then in use to around 5,000 kilometres. The tank had a new engine design (the V-26) and new transmission, and was a well-sorted machine that became known as Obiekt-167. But no matter what actions Kartsev took – or indeed how

ABOVE A column of T-55A tanks during Soviet Army manoeuvres.

ABOVE RIGHT A column of T-55 tanks moving along a track during a Soviet exercise. Note the KMT plough/dozer mounting points and the clipped track guards.

badly the Obiekt-432 performed on test – the Technical Council refused to accept the new alternative tank design, and turned it down at every stage of development. Even a turbine-powered version, the Obiekt-167T, was seen as not acceptable, even though the technology predated the later T-80 tank design by an entire decade.

After the Obiekt-432 tank was accepted for service, Kartsev was summarily told by the then Technical Council President Dmitry Ustinov that the improved Obiekt-434 version (subsequently designated as the T-64A as the Obiekt-432 became the T-64) would be the only new standard tank and that all of the tank plants would build this design. But as the T-64 and T-64A were still suffering mightily from their 5TD-based engines, it was nevertheless proposed that the UVZ develop a 'mobilization' version of that tank, powered by a more conventional tried and tested V-2 type engine. Kartsev and his chief assistant, V. I. Venediktov, took up the project and designated it Obiekt-172. The results were awful: the Technical Council disliked the T-64A autoloader, the running gear, tracks, and many other details about the

BELOW LEFT The 'guitara' sectioned to show the gear arrangement inside.
BELOW RIGHT The gear change mechanism; note that 7 and 8 are solid rods, not hoses or cables.
BOTTOM The complete driveline with torsion bars and suspension arms as well as one of the lever-action shock absorbers on wheel station 5. Note first four suspension arms are trailing link and fifth one is leading link.

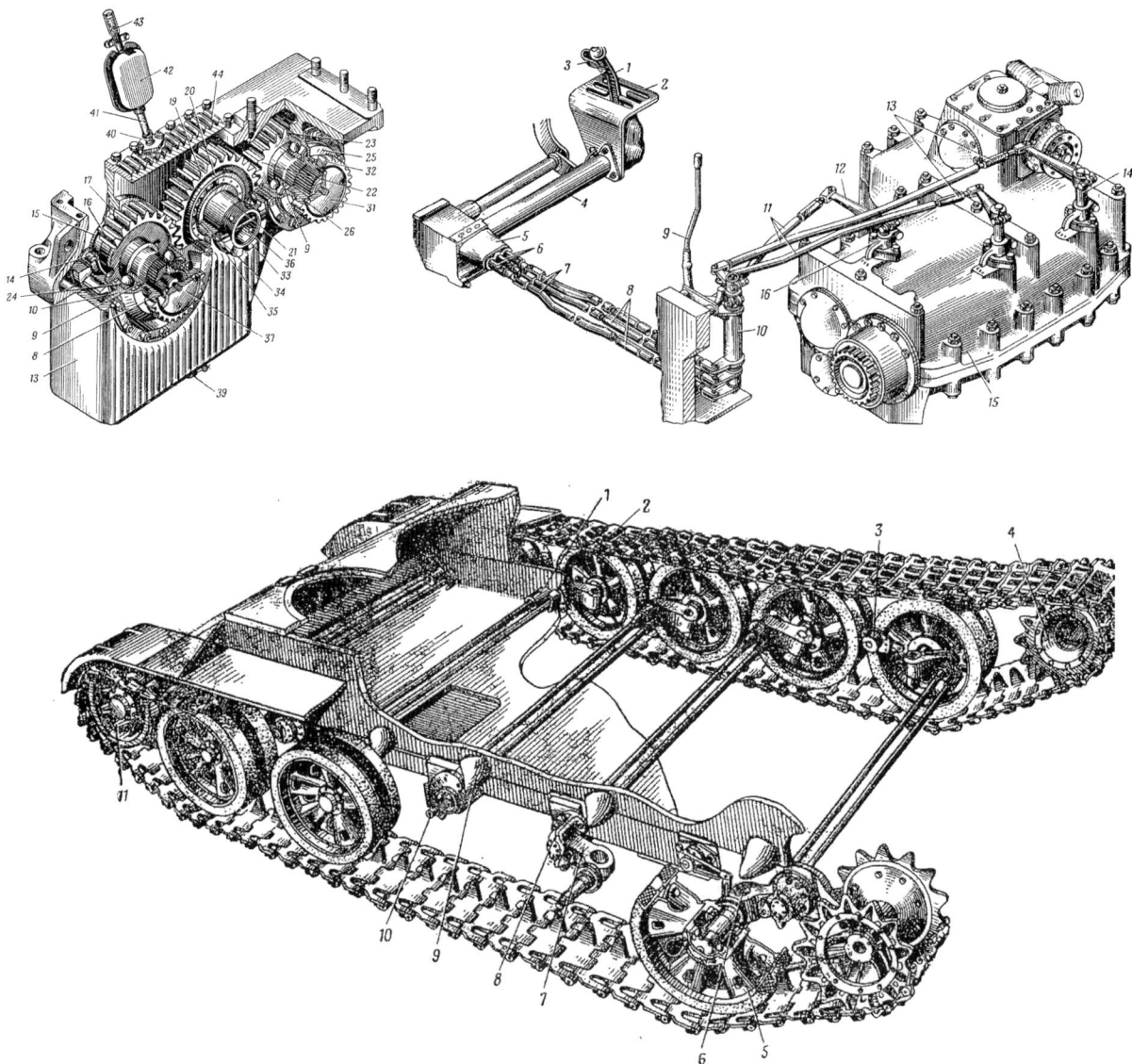

tank. So Kartsev asked if they could make some 'minor' modifications to the design to make it easier to produce. They received permission and…

The Obiekt-172M was a completely new tank that only superficially resembled the T-64A. Fitted with a new stern to accommodate the V-45 engine and transfer case to match the 7-speed Kharkov-built transmissions mounted on each side, the tank now bore the running gear and tracks from the stillborn Obiekt-167 tank and also the brand-new 'Zhelud' autoloader, using cassettes, which was much safer than the open storage 'cabin' type developed in Kharkov.

Ustinov and his acolytes were furious, and as a result Kartsev was 'promoted' to an inspectorate job while Venediktov took over the design bureau at the end of 1969. Ustinov was unamused that he was now being forced to test the new tank alongside his beloved T-64A, as well as an upstart turbine-powered version of the T-64A developed by Leningrad as the Obiekt-219 Sp2. Both tanks proved superior to the T-64A no matter what testing Ustinov ordered, and when he was on holiday in 1972 the military had the Obiekt-172M signed into production as the T-72 main battle tank (MBT). It speaks volumes that after the Soviet Union collapsed, the Russian Federation kept most of the Obiekt-172M (T-72) and Obiekt-219 Sp2 (T-80) derivative tanks and gave many of their T-64 tanks back to newly independent Ukraine. The exchange was logical both from a national perspective but also very much from a maintenance perspective, with T-72 production having been in Russia and T-64 production in Ukraine, with only the T-80 split between manufacturing plants located in both countries.

Kartsev received a number of awards and decorations as well as military promotion to General-Major, but never got to work on tank designs again. He died in Moscow on 13 April 2013. His approach was always an evolutionary one, adding welcome changes where needed but not including unproven or risky technology that could fail without warning. Kartsev's three series production tank designs, the T-55, T-62 and T-72, all continue to serve today, with the current T-90 also being a development of the T-72. The Kartsev legacy Soviet tanks, not least the T-55, are still considered iconic tanks of the Cold War era, and remain current today in many parts of the world.

OPPOSITE TOP Layout of electrical components in the hull of the T-55 showing their location and the simplicity of the wiring system used for those items.
OPPOSITE BOTTOM Layout of the electrical components in the original Model 1958 T-55 tank. This became much more involved with the M series upgrades in the 1980s and new sights, sensors and equipment being added.

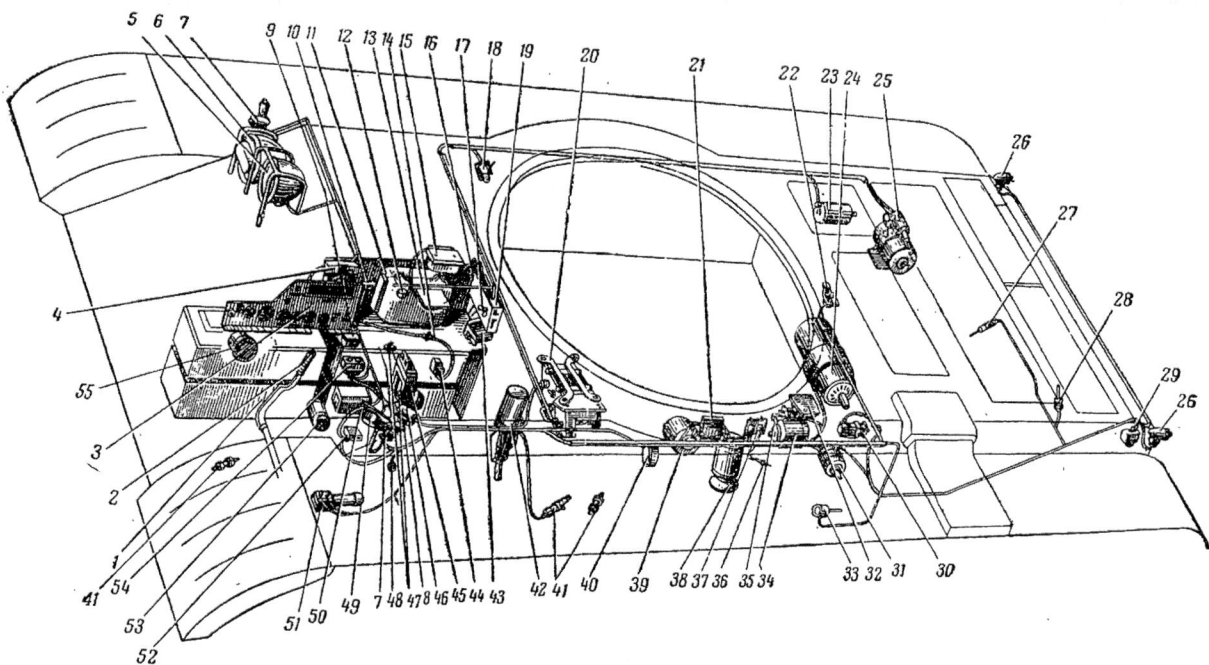

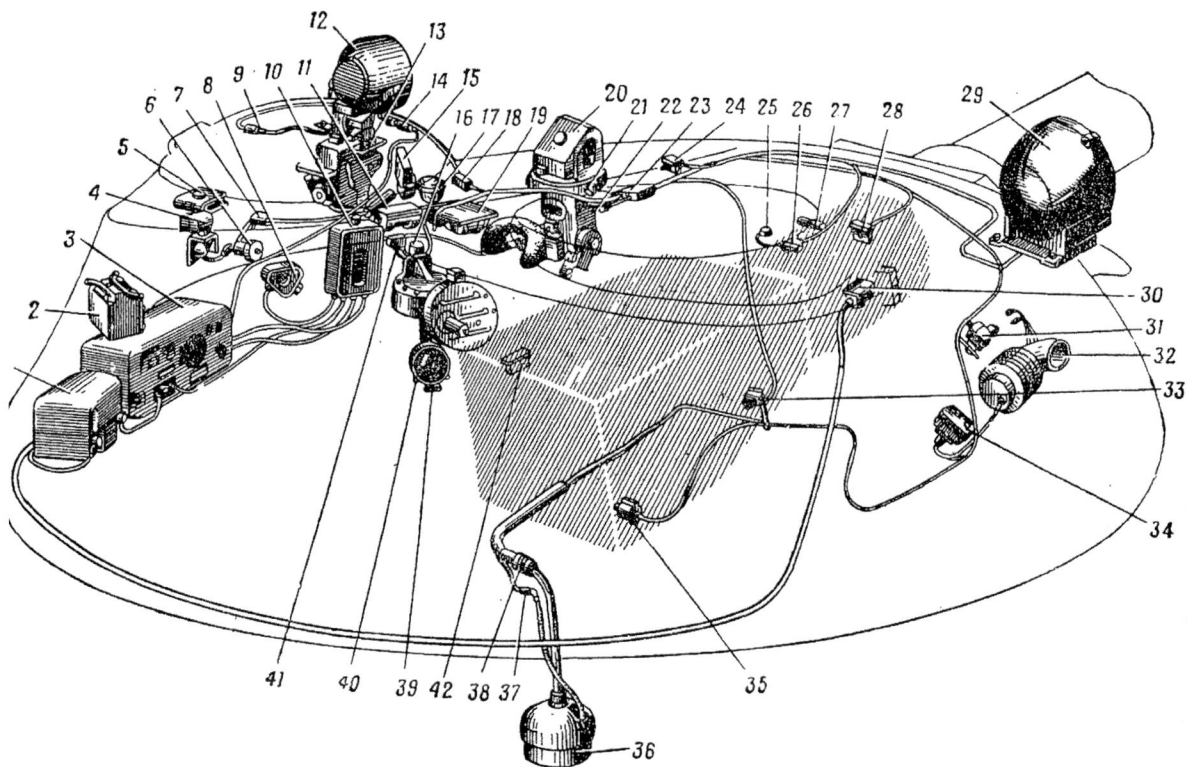

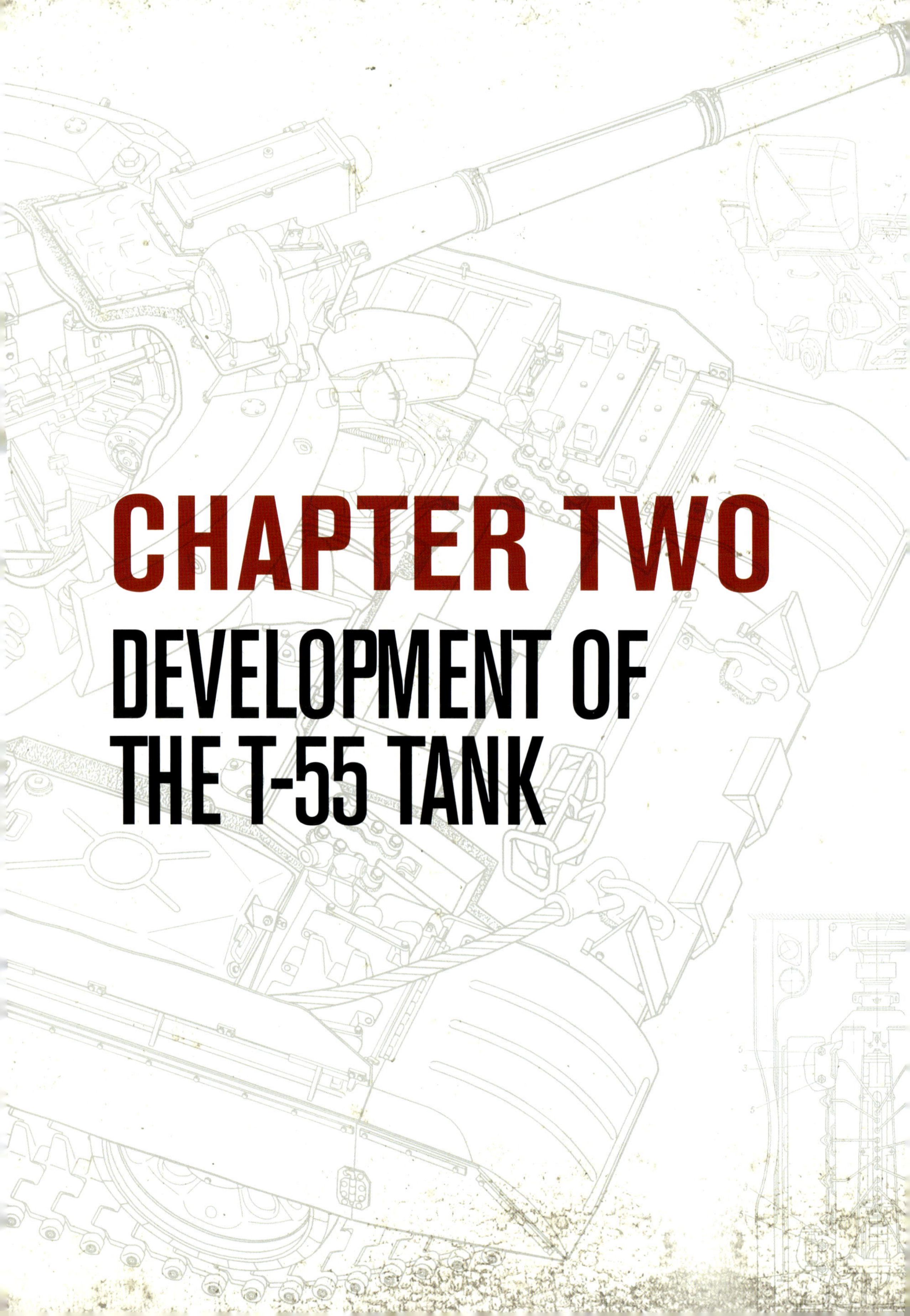

CHAPTER TWO

DEVELOPMENT OF THE T-55 TANK

KARTSEV ARRIVES

Unlike the T-54, which took six years from completion of the first prototypes to the first major production series with the T-54 Model 1951, the developmental curve for the T-55 was much shorter. Leonid Kartsev had taken over as the chief designer of the Ural Railway Wagon Construction Plant (UVZ) in 1953, and he had been initially responsible for the development of the T-54A and T-54B tanks.

Kartsev, together with several other new graduates, had arrived at the UVZ in 1949 straight out of the Military Academy of the Armed Forces as a newly minted captain of engineers. He began as a transmission designer under A. I. Shpaykhler and began work on the steering mechanism for the T-54. From there, he went on to work on the BTS-2 (Bronyevoy Tyagach Sredny or Sredny Tankovy Tyagach – Medium Tank Tractor) recovery vehicle, specifically on the power take-off from the 'guitara' transfer case and associated hydraulic pump for the high-speed winch. He became a 'rationalizer' or problem solver along with V. I. Venediktov, who would be his friend and close confidant until he left UVZ in 1969.

One of their first projects together was redesigning the engine heater assembly for the T-54. There was a 'political' problem in that this device had been designed personally by then chief designer A. A. Morozov, who was intolerant of subordinate engineers deviating from his designs. While he was ill at the time of this redesign, when he returned he would surely not permit them to try their design in metal. So they pulled 'a fast one' on him. They had him sign off on pencil sketches versus blueprints as part of a new heater assembly for the engine. When they built and tested it, the new design was very successful and entered series production.

Morozov was then sent to Moscow in 1951 for an operation for stomach ulcers. In December 1951 he was renamed as head of the reformed design bureau in Kharkov, and the temporary UVZ chief designer was named as A. V. Kolesnikov. He was at the time 54 years old, but had been one of Mikhail Koshkin's deputies in Kharkov working on the T-34 in the late 1930s. Although Kolesnikov headed up work on series production of the T-54 medium tank during 1952–53, he was not, however, confirmed to be the new chief designer.

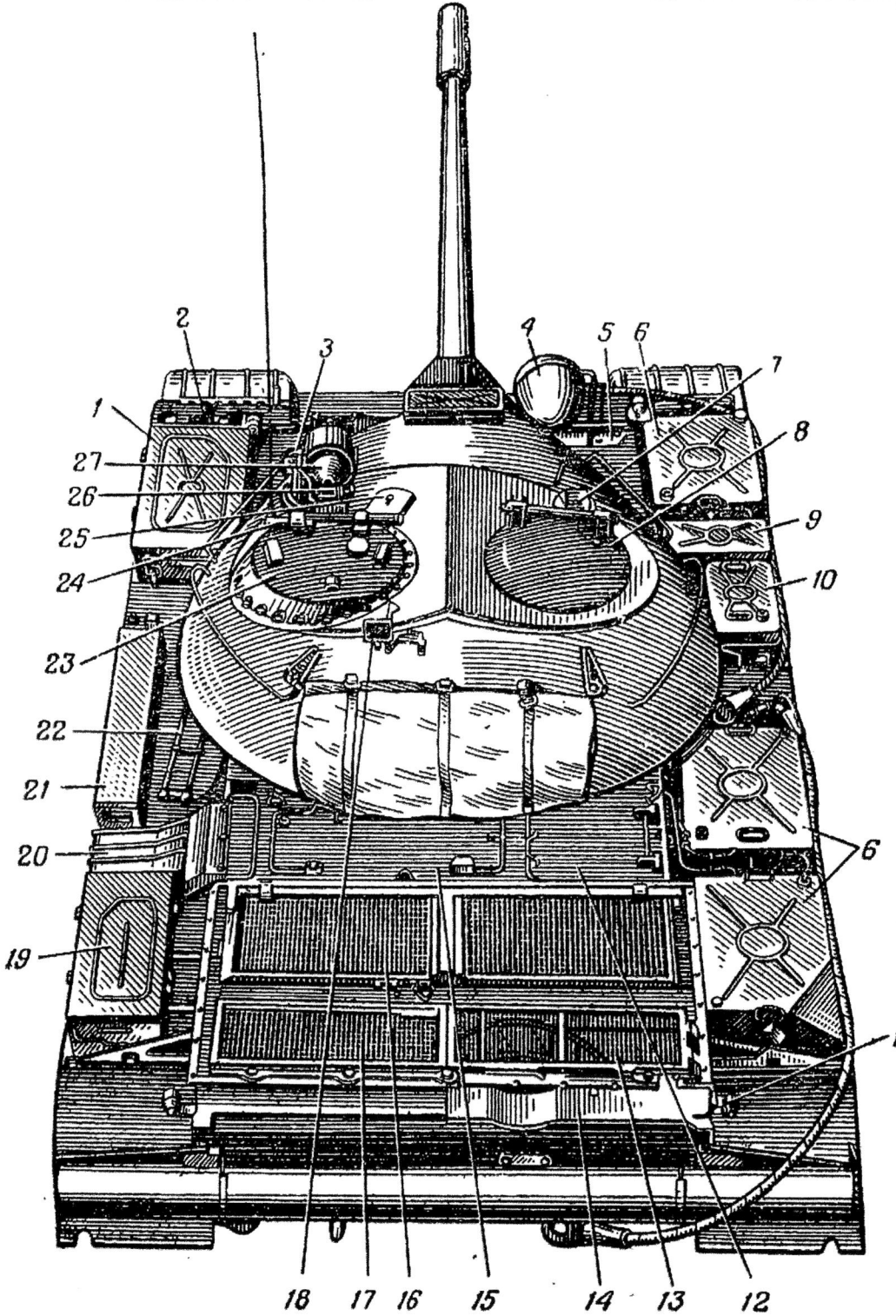

OPPOSITE Top view from the rear of the Model 1958 showing the overall layout of the tank, including the oil tank on the right fender in front of the rear fuel tanks and the garrison stowage tarpaulin stowed on the rear of the turret.
ABOVE Layout of the driver-mechanic's compartment in the T-55 prior to the M model changeover to the suspended driver-mechanic's seat. The seat back is down and the air tanks on the left and two 250-round 7.62mm ammunition cans can be seen on the right.

In January 1953 Leonid Kartsev was named as the chief designer for the 'Gorizont' single-axis stabilizer system for what became the T-54A modification. Kartsev was soon called up to meet with plant manager I. N. Okunev, who asked him, 'Know anything about tanks?' Kartsev answered, 'Perhaps I do. Graduated with honours from a tank school in 1942, served as a tank mechanic at the front, and after the war graduated from the Armoured Academy with a Gold Medal. Now working here for four years in the tank design bureau.' Okunev then sent him to meet with the Chief of the Industrial Section of the Sverdlovsk Party Committee of the Communist Party of the Soviet Union (CPSU), Comrade Gryaznov. After a pleasant meeting with him, Kartsev was sent to Moscow to meet with the chief of 'Glavtank' (Main Directorate for Tank Building of the MTrM of the USSR) N. A. Kucherenko.

ABOVE The fighting compartment (turret) interior with the gunner's position forward and the commander's seat behind him, R-113 radio set at his left elbow.

RIGHT Engine compartment arrangement with the air cleaner at the upper left, fan at the upper right, and oil cooler radiator at the bottom centre.

After meeting with Kucherenko, they went to see the Deputy Minister of the MTrM, S. A. Makhonin. Finally, they then met with Minister Yu. Ye. Maksarev. The next day they went to meet with the Chief of Defence Production of the Central Committee of the CPSU, I. D. Serbin. However, after that meeting Kartsev was simply told to go home. Three weeks later he

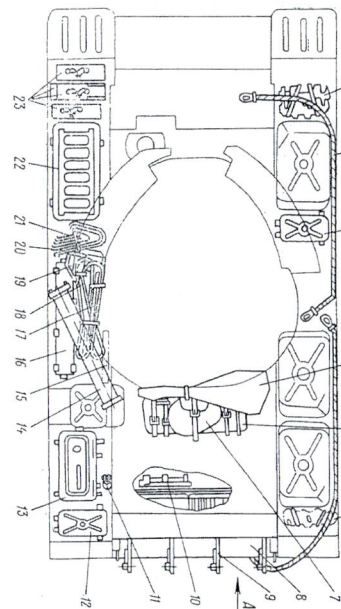

was called up to Okunev's office where he was informed 'per an Order from the Ministry you are designated as the Chief Designer for the (UVZ) Plant'. This was on 7 March 1953 – two days after the death of Ioseph Stalin. The appointment was confirmed by the Politburo in June 1953.

Kartsev took over Section 520, the design bureau, which at that time had 120 personnel working there. Kartsev noted many of them had not had any higher education but had risen through the ranks from the days of working in Kharkov on the BT tanks and the T-34. They had a very didactic methodology for working on tank designs, with a great deal of trial and error taking the place of actual research and engineering design. Kartsev felt that this was one reason there were problems with aspects of the T-54 tank's design and reliability.

During the war, Morozov had taken complete charge of all T-34 design work and improvements when as many as six different tank plants were assembling the T-34 and effectively building six different versions of the tank. Morozov knew from field service reports that parts from one tank plant were not necessarily interchangeable with another, so he managed to negotiate a formal instruction from Moscow that he would personally take control of the situation as sole designer of the tank, and, further, that all plans, blueprints and changes would henceforth go only through him. As a result, by 1951 he had established a very strict but rational order for preparing and producing technical documentation. Several versions could be offered, but it was only after either Morozov or one of his trusted deputies agreed with the work that the blueprints would be produced for production.

ABOVE LEFT A tank crew removing the engine deck of a T-55. Note the mounting locations of the unditching log and OPVT snorkel.

TOP Outer vehicle materials (OVM) stowage on the T-55 tanks, with the later three-section snorkel (14) in place at the left rear of the turret.

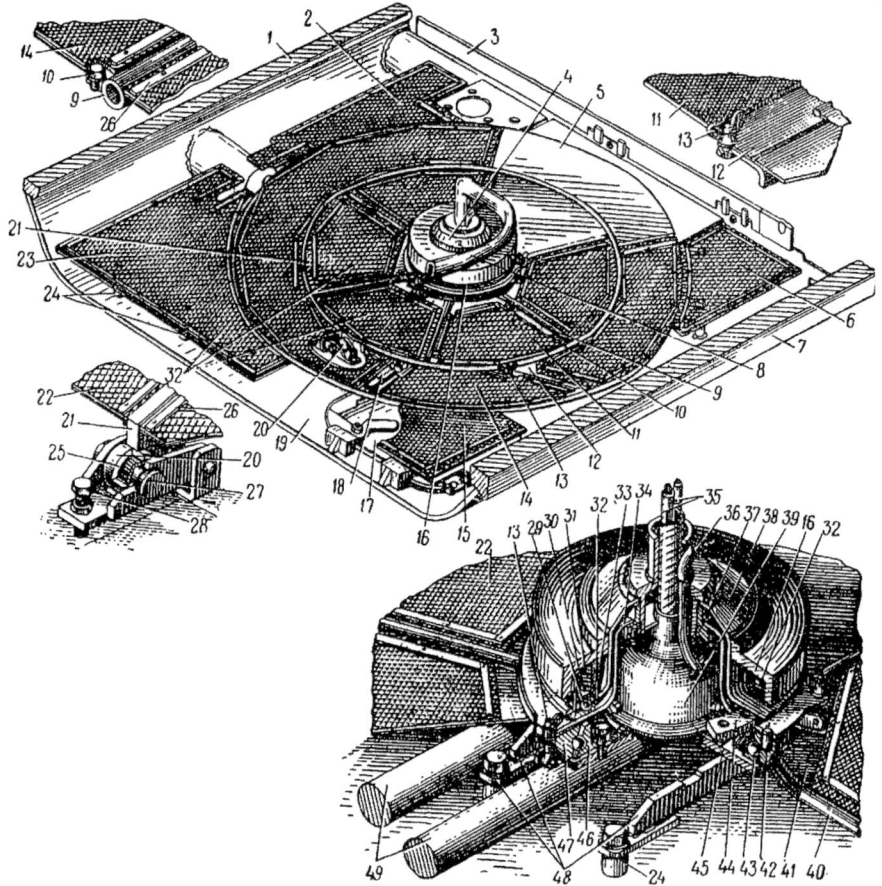

Another solution they came up with was giving each tank a number, which was internal to the tank plant for design development purposes – the 'Obiekt' or Object number. The T-34-85 became Obiekt-135, the T-44 Obiekt-136, and the T-54 became Obiekt-137. This permitted better grouping of all of the documentation and blueprints.

Now in charge at UVZ in Nizhny Tagil, Kartsev handed over the design of the 'Gorizont' to a classmate from the Academy, Yu. A. Kovalev. But soon after that, the NKVD (Narodny Kommissariat Vnutrenikh Del, Peoples' Commissariat for Internal Affairs) paid him a visit with the declaration that 'too many Jews are working in your design bureau. We will remove them.' This anti-Jewish sentiment had followed on from concerns emanating from Stalin himself, culminating in what was called 'The Doctor's Plot', which came to a head at the time of Stalin's own death. Kartsev vociferously protested as these engineers were the backbone of the design cadre and their loss would cripple the plant. Fortunately, before that event took place

Lavrenty P. Beria, the head of the NKVD, was himself arrested, with the direct involvement of the Soviet Army under Marshal of the Soviet Union Georgy K. Zhukov, and the request was quietly dropped.

Once things settled down, Kartsev started work on the BTS-4 tank recovery vehicle, for which the winch mechanism design was proving a technical challenge. Another problem involved the 'guitara' transfer case in service tanks, which had been running reliably for up to 10,000 kilometres in these tanks but was now beginning to fail. The solution was in using a different grade of steel. Also, the T-54 turret drive had difficulty operating if the tank was tilted around 15° in either direction, so that too needed to be fixed. But over time all these problems were overcome. In 1955, Kartsev reported to the chief of GBTU (Gosudarstvennoye Bronetankirovannoye Upravleniye – Main Armoured Vehicle Directorate), General-Lieutenant I. A. Lebedev, that they were making up to 3,000 changes to the blueprints of the T-54 per year with an average of 10 commensurate changes daily in the design of components. Kartsev also had to deal with such foolish proposals as having the same basic issue item tools for the T-54 as provided to the T-10, a much larger and more complex tank. He turned such proposals down.

At the end of 1953 Kartsev was summoned to Moscow and given a task to work on the next Soviet medium tank, as was Morozov, who had been called from Kharkov. The new generation tank was to have a combat weight of 36 metric tonnes, be armed with the new D-54TS high-power 100mm rifled gun and have engine power output increased from 520hp in the T-54 to 580hp, using the same well-proven V-2 type engine as the existing tank. Engine-designer I. Ya. Trashutin considered such an increase in horsepower was possible, and assigned engineers to the task. The new tank, now designated Obiekt-140, was a primary design bureau occupation at UVZ in 1954–55. To take overall care of the project, Kartsev appointed another classmate, V. I. Venediktov, to handle the design work on the Obiekt-140 project. Venediktov would soon also be named as one of Kartsev's primary deputies.

The new tank design, while shaping up, was not, however, a massive leap forward from the current T-54, and after several sleepless nights Kartsev sent a letter to the Council of Ministers of the USSR (Sovet Ministrov, SM SSSR) asking them to cancel the undertaking. The plant had spent 16 million roubles on the project, and while the prototypes worked well and showed promise, they were not such a major advance over the T-54 as would warrant retooling the plant and the consequent disruption this would cause. Kartsev took the 'blame' personally, and to deflect blame from Venediktov recommended that his assistant go to China to help set up the production line that would eventually result in the Type 59 medium tank derived from the Soviet T-54.

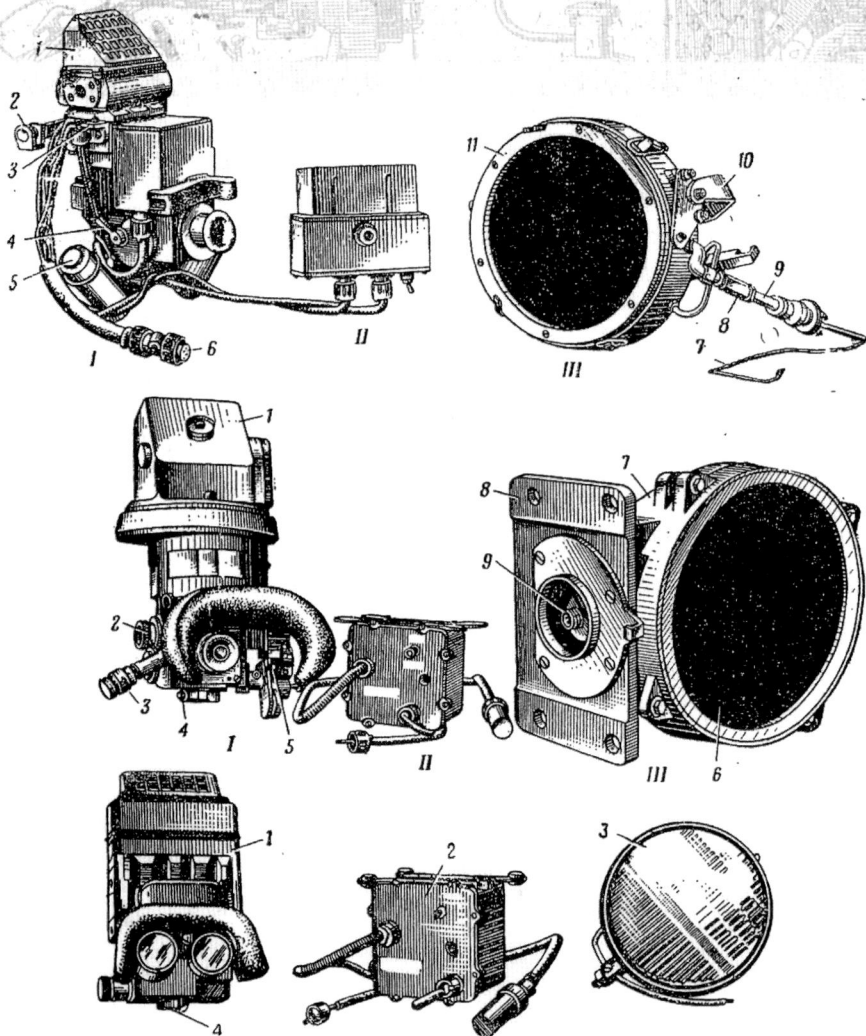

At the same time (1954–55) Kartsev and the plant also worked on parallel research into single-axis and twin-axis stabilization for the T-54 main armament. A third task was the development of underwater driving equipment (Oborudovaniye Podvodnoy Vozhdeniya Tanki, OPVT) for the T-54. Some furious arguments took place over the gun stabilizers with the plant chief engineer, A. V. Volkov, who was vehemently against the principle being proposed. Problems did occur: while testing the single-axis (vertical stabilizer) the deputy chief designer of the system, F. N. Avdeyev, was crushed between the gun breech and the turret wall when the stabilizer levelled the gun, simultaneously cracking the skull of A. S. Lipkin located in front of the tank. Both men survived the incident, but with serious injuries.

Development and testing, though not straightforward, did ultimately result in a workable solution, and the T-54A entered series production, followed by the T-54B with the twin-axis 'Tsiklon' stabilizer a year later. The first problem encountered with the T-54B in service was increased wear on the turret race gear teeth caused by the movement of the stabilizer in the horizontal axis. This required additional heat treatment (hardening) during manufacture to prevent breakage under use. As none of the state ball-bearing factories were able to produce precise enough bearings to use with this device, UVZ began to make its own bearings for their turret races, a not inconsiderable investment.

ENTER THE T-55 TANK

The T-55 tank was Kartsev's attempt to combine all of the latest proven measures in Soviet tank design into one tank design, and the T-54 was the perfect canvas on which to paint all of them at one time.

The ChTZ plant (Chelyabinsky Traktorny Zavod imeni V.I. Lenina) in Chelyabinsk had developed a new fire suppression system (Potivo-Pozharnoye Oborudovaniye, PPO) for their T-10 tank, but the designers in Leningrad responsible for the tank refused to let them introduce it (apparently for one of the oldest technical design reasons – 'not invented here'). So the system designer, a man named Silchenko, offered it to Kartsev at UVZ in Nizhny Tagil. After testing in the T-54 it was adopted for their improved tank as the 'Roza' system.

Also now appearing was a thermal smoke generating system (Termal'naya Dymovaya Apparata, TDA), which used diesel fuel directly injected into the exhaust manifold to create a dense cloud of smoke. This was better than the use of the BDSh-5 canisters carried on the T-54, while it also freed up the rear of the tank for permanent installation of racks to carry two 200-litre auxiliary fuel tanks. The TDA system was also adopted for service.

The latest systems developed for the T-54B, namely the infrared sights and searchlights, and the underwater driving equipment (OPVT) were also improved and became integral to the design of the new tank.

While the Obiekt-140 had not passed muster, its new engine, now dubbed the V-55, was now available and provided 580hp versus the 520hp of the V-54. At the end of 1955, the new tank design acquired the designator Obiekt-155.

The 'stellazh' forward ammunition racks from the T-54 were also redesigned to a 'wet' design with fuel cells wrapping around the individual ammunition sleeves. With other changes, a total of 680 litres of fuel was now stowed under armour within the tank; combined with 285 litres in three external tanks and 400 litres carried in the auxiliary tanks, this gave the new tank a highway range of up to 700 kilometres.

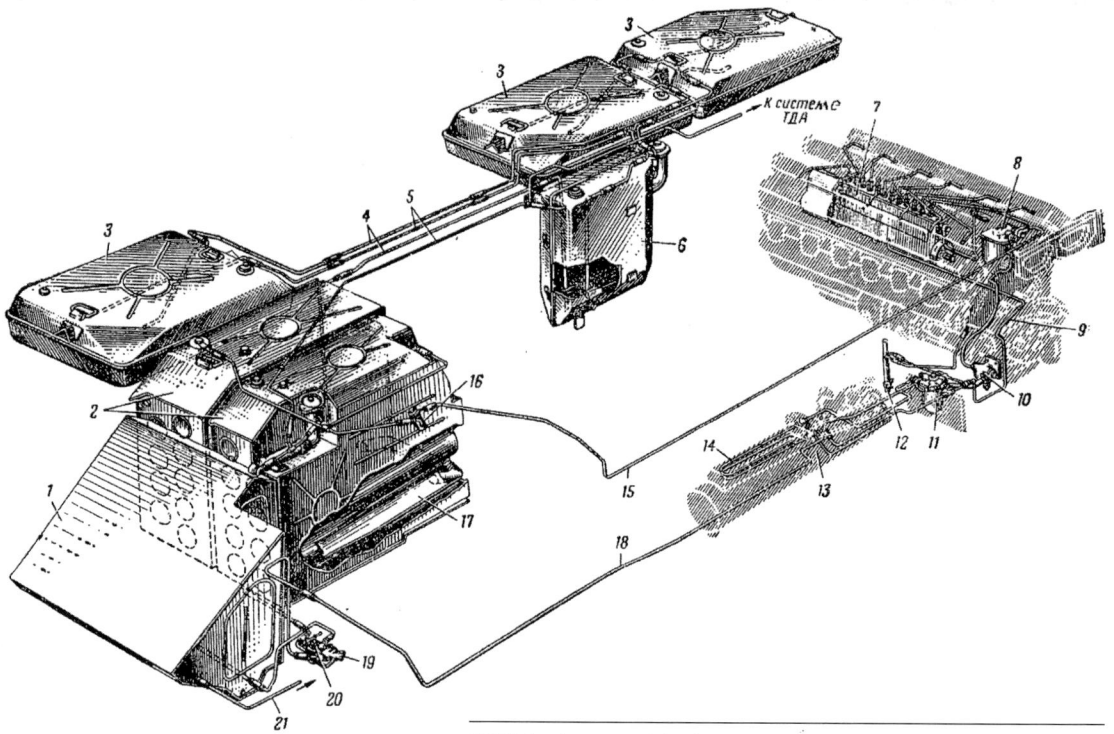

ABOVE A schematic of the fuel system of the T-55 showing the twin 'stellazh' tanks in the bow, main tank on the right side of the engine compartment, three external fuel tanks, and the feed piping to the engine and the engine pre-heater.

BELOW LEFT Two three-quarter views of the V-55 version of the V-2 diesel engine, which produced 580hp in its initial version.

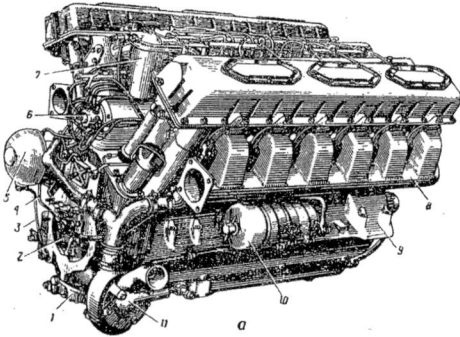

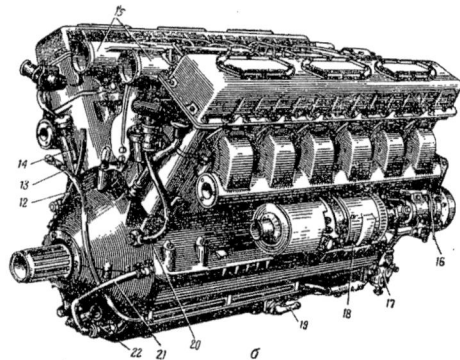

While this was going on, testing by troop units and other Soviet research institutes showed that the 12.7mm DShKM anti-aircraft machine gun (AAMG) of the T-54 was of little use against the new generation of low-flying jet engine aircraft. The wartime Soviet 'Shturmovik' propeller-driven ground attack aircraft was now out of service and its role in the Soviet Air Force was taken by MiG-17 and Su-7 fighter-bombers, with similar developments in all foreign air forces. As a result, the new tank eliminated the effectively redundant loader's AAMG cupola and fittings, replacing them with a simple domed hatch.

The new Soviet tank design also benefited from other research. Since exploding its first atomic bomb in 1949, the Soviet Union had carried out extensive research with

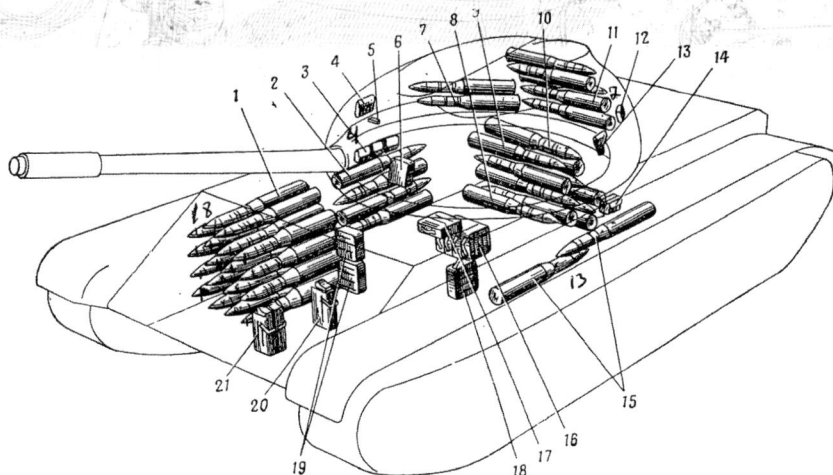

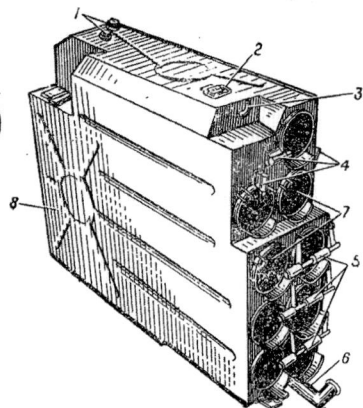

ABOVE The ammunition stowage arrangement of the T-55s, which only really varied with the M models or command tanks. There are 20 rounds in the 'stellazh' racks, 4 on the right side, 2 on the left, 2 on the back, 9 on the firewall and 6 in the turret for a total of 43.
RIGHT The left (top) and right (lower) 'stellazh' fuel tanks removed from the tank. Each one holds ten 100mm rounds.
BOTTOM A cross-section of the later production and upgraded 14-tooth drive wheels, showing the addition of a track-tooth guide to assist in preventing thrown tracks.

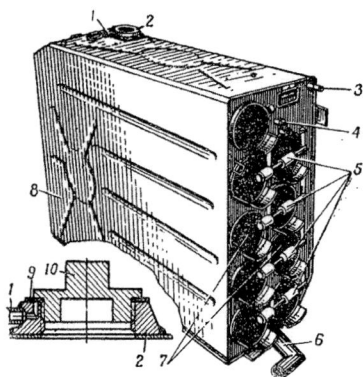

nuclear weapons at the Semipalatinsk test range. It was found that with low-yield nuclear weapons (2–15 Kt) a T-54 tank could survive if it was 1,500 metres or further away from ground zero. While a bit simplistic, as it ignored the multiple criteria used to determine nuclear effects – burst height, quality of the weapon, boosters used, type of terrain, etc. – Soviet designers felt that if they could provide the crew with an element of anti-atomic protection (Protivoatomnoi Zashiti – PAZ) the tank could survive temporarily on a nuclear battlefield.

The new tank was redesigned to be hermetically sealed, with a filter and centrifugal blower to provide clean air for the crew while also creating overpressure inside the tank's inhabited sections to keep radioactive dust out of the tank. This called for a complete redesign of the ventilation system, the most obvious external feature being the removal of the mushroom-shaped ventilator on the turret roof. It also assisted in relieving a common problem in Soviet tanks of the day, namely propellant gas build-up in the turret.

The tank also had a major upgrade in its ammunition complement, with a total of 43 rounds being carried versus the 34 round complement of all early T-54 line tanks. Achieving this additional ammunition stowage required 11 rounds to be stowed on the floor in front of the hull firewall, and care had to

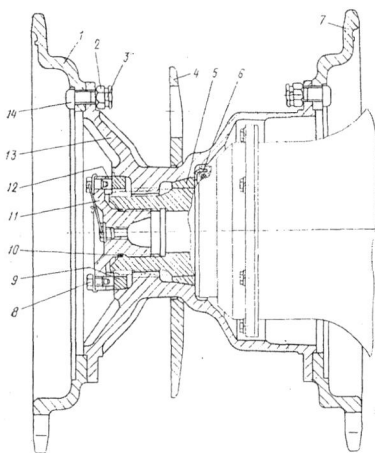

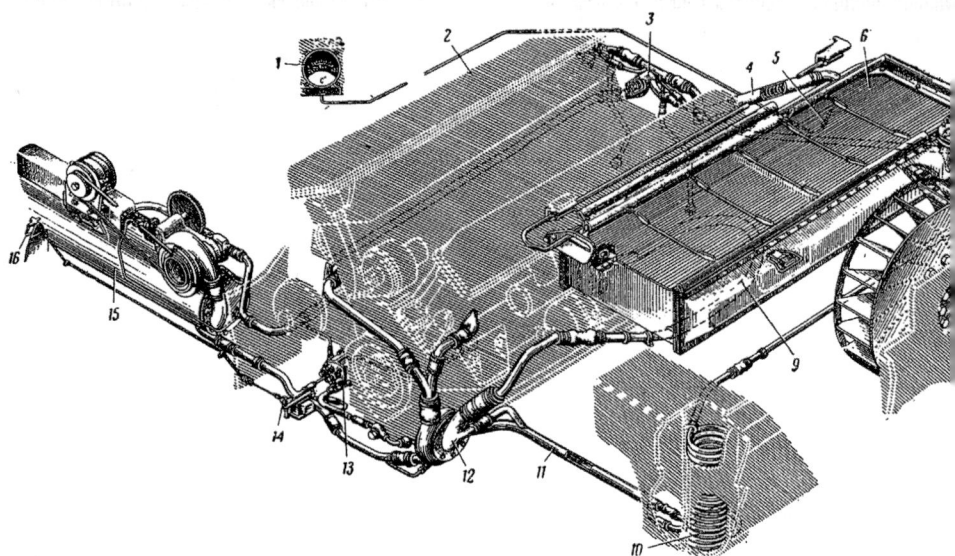

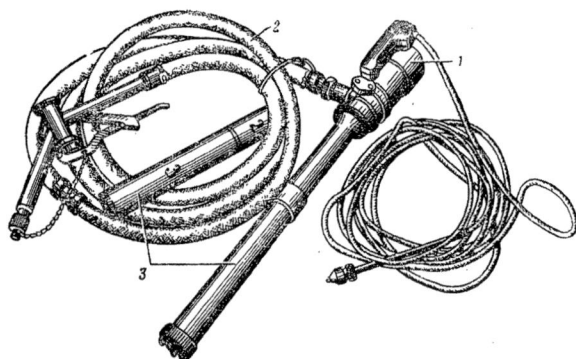

be taken in locking them in place and then unlocking them from their racks for use. The tank also retained the rotating turret floor introduced on the T-54B.

The new tank design successfully passed all of its state tests with flying colours, and in the middle of 1957 it was accepted for service as the T-55, with formal adoption taking place in May 1958, full production actually having already begun on 1 January 1958. One of the reasons for this delay was purely bureaucratic: all of the ministries were required to comply with the Councils of National Economy (Sovnarkhozov), and local manufacturing plants had to work through and with those organizations, which was always a slow bureaucratic process that ran behind the actual design and production process.

Series production of the new T-55 tank took place at Nizhny Tagil (Uralvagonzavod – UVZ), Kharkov (Plant No. 75) and Omsk (Plant No. 174, formally Leningrad Voroshilov Plant or LVZ). Production continued at UVZ from 1958 until about 1972, when it was replaced in production there by the T-72; Kharkov appears to have produced the T-55 series from 1958 to about 1969, when the T-64A entered full series production, and only Omsk produced the T-55 continuously from 1958 to

1979, when the plant switched over to T-80 tank production.*

There were inevitably some teething problems in initial production. For instance, as the first production T-55 tanks were being assembled, it was found that the fuel filler cap and the fuel filler pipe throat for the central fuel tank were not aligned. One of the designers, A. S. Serikov, was responsible for the mistake. When the factory director called for him, they found he was at a chess tournament in Sverdlovsk. He was recalled and the technical issue was quickly sorted out.

CONCERNS ABOUT NUCLEAR WARFARE – STAGE 1

By the end of the 1950s, the Soviet Union had fielded its first medium range ballistic missile system, the R-5M, with the larger and longer-range R-12 and R-14 soon to enter service. After initially trailing the United States in the field of nuclear weapons development and the means to deliver such weapons to target, the Soviet Union had caught up during the 1950s, such that by the beginning of the 1960s tactical planning now also had to consider the potential of conflict in a nuclear contaminated zone. Soviet testing of nuclear warfare doctrine in order to develop tactics and weapons systems to conduct warfare within such a nuclear environment showed that there would be inevitable operational problems with the first tanks that would be required to take and hold the 'ground zero' sites where nuclear weapons had been used. Soviet doctrine originally factored that tanks would sweep across contaminated areas in less than 20 minutes, but then considered that within certain contaminated 'hot' zone scenarios, the first tanks and other armoured vehicles would have to stay there longer than originally envisaged. Tank crews would therefore need significantly more protection to survive within that environment.

With a view to protecting tank crews from contaminated dust particles being drawn into the tank by the fighting compartment and engine ventilation and cooling systems, an anti-atomic protection system (designated PAZ in Russian) was developed for all tanks based on Soviet Ministry of Defence Order No. 75

---

* One of the authors encountered one of the last Omsk-built T-55s at Camp Grayling, Michigan, in August 1984. It bore 1979 production markings and stamped dates on all of the key components requiring them, but in actuality was probably a Model 1969 tank that had undergone capital rebuilding in that year. There was no information available as to where it came from, but the supposition was that it had been captured in Lebanon by the IDF and sent to the US for evaluation. Most of the ancillary items such as the radio set and machine guns had been removed from the tank and it had all crew hatches and access hatches fixed open to include the engine, radiator and air cleaner sections. The tank was undamaged. It has since been removed.

RIGHT A schematic view of the left final drive mechanism and the band or strap type of brakes used for slowing the tank.
BELOW The layout of the components of the PAZ atomic protection system within the turret. There is a pneumatic seal and plugs for the bow and turret machine guns, telescopic sight, and an overpressure fan motor on the left side of the turret.

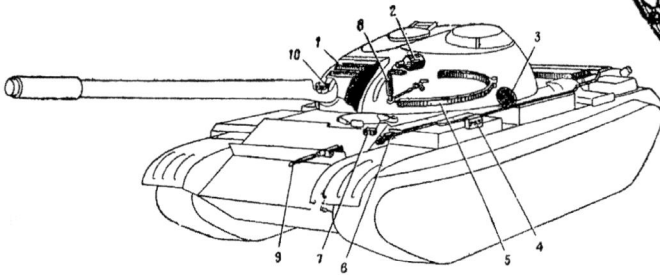

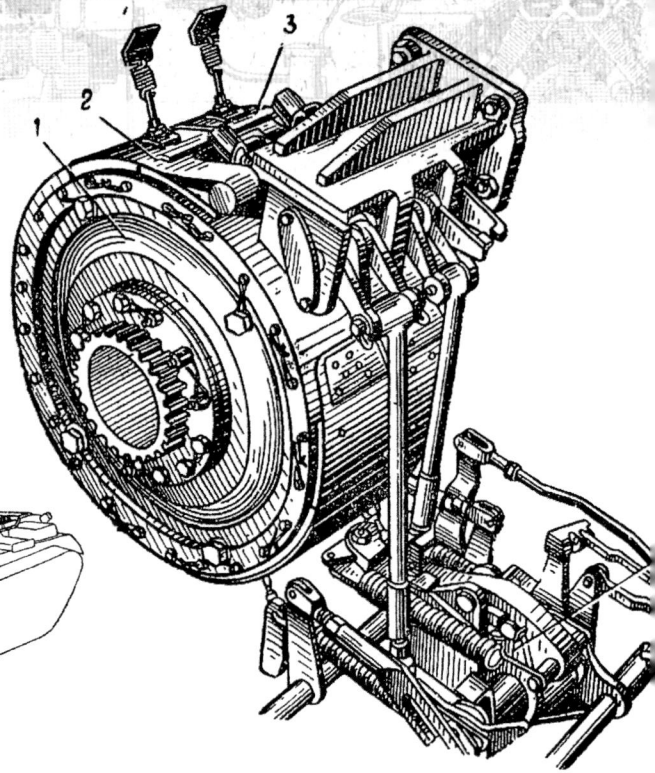

dated 1 April 1959. The PAZ system developed for the T-55 was undertaken at Plant No. 75 in Kharkov, consisting primarily of a pump that over-pressured the ambient air in the tank by 0.3MPa (3kg/cm^2), thereby keeping radioactive dust out of the tank. There were also elements of internal and external screening, which were further developed at Plant No. 174 and Plant No. 183.

CONCERNS ABOUT NUCLEAR WARFARE – STAGE 2

In the late 1950s, Soviet scientists had developed a hydrogen-impregnated plastic designated POV-20/POV-50S, which was found to reduce or stop neutron radiation, and hence in tank design terms to prevent radiation penetrating into the occupied areas of the tank. Experiments were conducted and it was found that if a liner (*podboy*) was made using this material it dramatically increased the protection of the crew. However, not all parts of the tank could be protected with this liner. The solution was thereby to use an appliqué version (*nadboy*) over certain parts of the tank, such as the hatches and hatch coamings, and on the centre roof section between the two hatch coamings. Prototype work on tanks with the combination of internal and external liners was undertaken at Plant No. 174 and Plant No. 183 in 1961, with the POV anti-radiation material being produced at the Safronovsky plant in Smolensk Oblast.

As was the norm in the Soviet Union, two independent tank designs with nuclear protection were developed and tested in competition, with the results being an amalgamation of the efforts of both design bureaus. In accordance with Resolution TsK KPSS (Tsentral'ny Komitet Kommunicheskoy Partii Sovetskogo Soyuza, Central Committee of the Communist Party of the Soviet Union) SM No. 141-58 dated 17 February 1961, OKB-174 at Plant No. 174 in Omsk under the direction of A. A. Morov developed the Obiekt-607 prototype with strengthened anti-atomic (anti-radiation) protection. Meanwhile, parallel development at the KB (Konstruktorskoye Byuro – Design Bureau) of Plant No. 183 (UVZ) in Nizhny Tagil under the direction of Yu. A. Levkovsky created the Obiekt-155A to fulfil the same design requirements. The Obiekt-155A was successfully tested in the last ten days of August 1961 near Tedzhent in the Turkmenistan Military District (TurkVO). The rival Obiekt-607 developed at Omsk was completed and tested towards the end of the year, the conclusions were made and elements of rework and design amalgamation were ordered based on the test report findings. Resolution No. 141-58 of the Council of Ministers of the Soviet Union (SM SSSR) dated 17 February

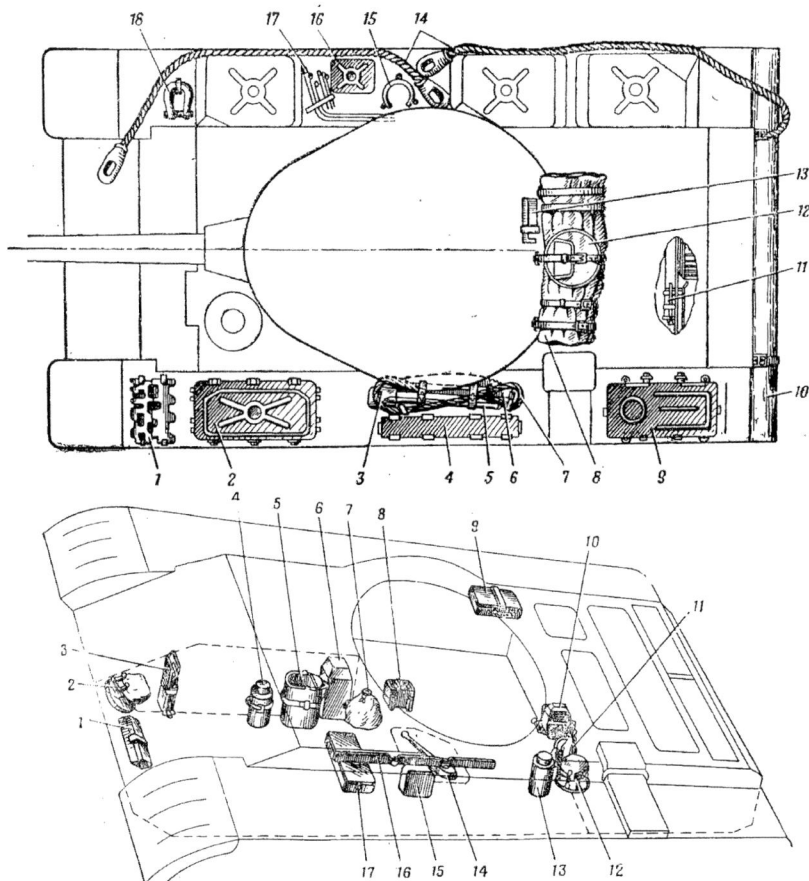

LEFT TOP ZIP (spare parts, tools and accessory) stowage on the outside of the T-55. The item inside the engine compartment is a grease gun.

LEFT BOTTOM ZIP stowage inside the hull of the T-55; 4 and 13 are water cans, 5 is a food can for transporting rations, and most of the remaining parts are spare elements for the TPK, TVN, and TKN devices.

1962 accepted the modified design for service with the Soviet Army as the T-55A. The corresponding Soviet Ministry of Defence (MO, Ministerstvo Oboroni) Order No. 92 dated 16 July 1962 ordered the production of both tank designs – or more likely an amalgamation of the best results from both efforts – as the Obiekt-155A (T-55A). The T-55A was produced as the Obiekt-155A at Plant No. 183 (UVZ) in Nizhny Tagil and as the 'Obiekt-607' (T-55A) at Plant No. 174 in Omsk from 1962 until as late as 1978. A small number of T-55A tanks were also built at the V. A. Malyshev plant in Kharkov from 1962 to 1965.

Thus in 1961 an improved version of the T-55, the T-55A, was introduced, which was fitted with this liner and appliqué, giving it a different external appearance. The cupola and hatches now had thick covers, which were essentially protective light metal shields for the liner material but which gave the tank a distinctive look with the bulkier hatch coamings.

Since not all T-55s would be sent forward into nuclear detonation zones, only about one tank in three or four was built as a T-55A variant. The tanks were built at the same three tank plants alongside the T-55, with series production running from 1963 to 1972 at UVZ in Nizhny Tagil, from 1963 to 1967 at Kharkov, and from 1963 to 1978 at Omsk. Plant No. 174 in Omsk later also developed and tested a T-55 prototype with increased *podboy* lining.

Although developed for warfare in a potential nuclear environment, the T-55A, as with all Soviet tanks, was never required to be operationally used in such a combat scenario. It would be 25 years later that the implications of actual combat in a nuclear contaminated zone would be tested, and in a civil emergency rather than a combat situation. When the Chernobyl No. 4 reactor exploded and melted down in 1986, the Soviet Union sent in various armoured vehicles, including a small number of T-64 tanks, to access the buildings concerned. T-64s near Chernobyl that were irradiated were stored there for 30 years, and just recently some were recommissioned for use in Donbass, but there are no reliable Russian records that the T-64 was actually used in the Chernobyl incident. These T-64 tanks were fitted with the same radiation liner as the T-55, as were the IMR (Inzhenirnaya Mashina Razgrazhdeniya) obstacle clearing engineer vehicles being used to inspect the damage and perform reconnaissance. The tanks and IMRs proved to have two massive shortcomings in such an environment.

One was that the liner was ineffective against high-density close-proximity neutron sources such as the destroyed core of a reactor, and the radiation penetrated into the inhabited parts of the vehicles irradiating the crew. The only solution was to remove all of the vision devices and seal the openings, fit the IMRs with lead sheeting for protection, and install remote control cameras for driving and evaluating the damage as well as operating the onboard equipment to try and clean up the area. Crews were also tightly limited in their time on station and essentially had less than 30 minutes per shift to work in the contaminated area.

Secondly, tanks and armoured vehicles are not really designed for easy decontamination, and radioactive dust and debris would lodge in places in the vehicles that were not accessible to normal decontamination measures. For many years the Nuclear, Biological, Chemical (NBC) Troops of the Soviet Army had fielded and prided themselves on their decontamination systems. Soviet AFVs were designed for temporary operation in a contaminated area whereas concurrent NATO tanks and armoured vehicles had no such protective measures, but fortunately such combat conditions were never put to the test during the Cold War. In a situation such as the Chernobyl incident the radiation protection proved ineffective, however. Vehicles were cleaned as best as possible and air cleaners were replaced after every work session, but the vehicles were left permanently irradiated and consequently had to be abandoned. Statistics vary significantly, but as many as 6,000 vehicles and pieces of equipment and a significant number of helicopters were left permanently abandoned in the fields near the reactor.

(As an aside, when the tanks were fielded in 1961 some Western experts claimed that the 'A' designation in T-55A meant 'atomic warfare version'. This was due to the poor intelligence available on Soviet tanks at the time and a failure to note that the Soviets, like the West, used sequential letters to show new versions of items. The first five letters of the Cyrillic alphabet, А, Б, В, Г, Д [A, B, V, G, D] were the most common ones.)

Upgraded T-55 Model 1972 tanks on exercise. The lead tank clearly shows it now mounts the KTD-1 laser range finder as well as being fitted with RMSh tracks.

TOP The components that make up the STP-2 'Tsiklon' twin-axis stabilizer for the main gun and co-axial machine gun.

BOTTOM The schematic of the installation of the 'Tsiklon' in the T-55, showing the connection of the rod to the tank's turret that controls the actual stabilization of the gun in the vertical axis as well as the other components.

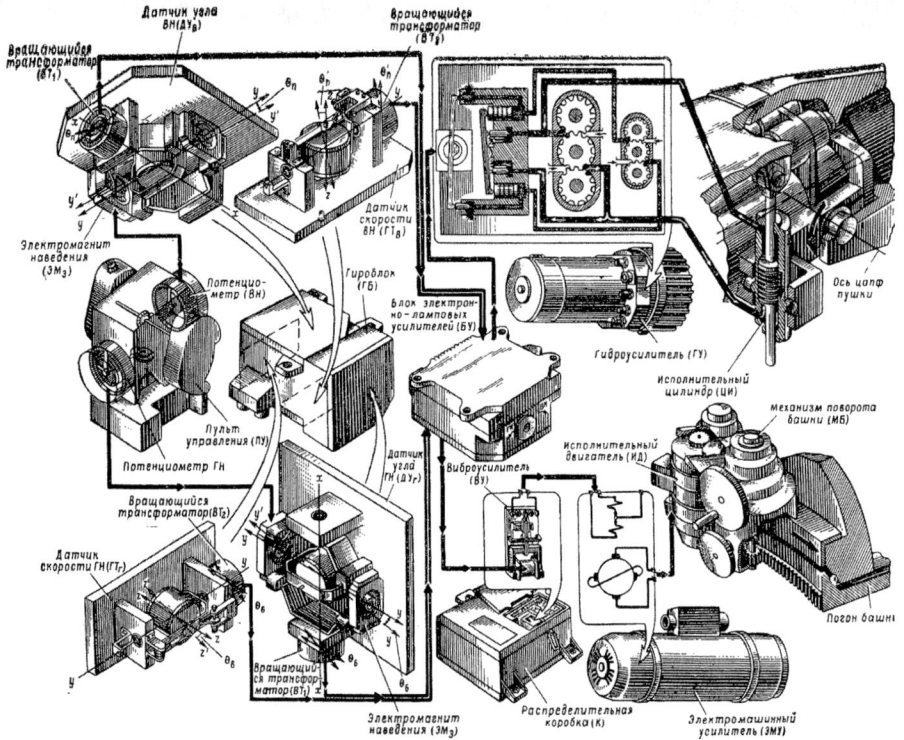

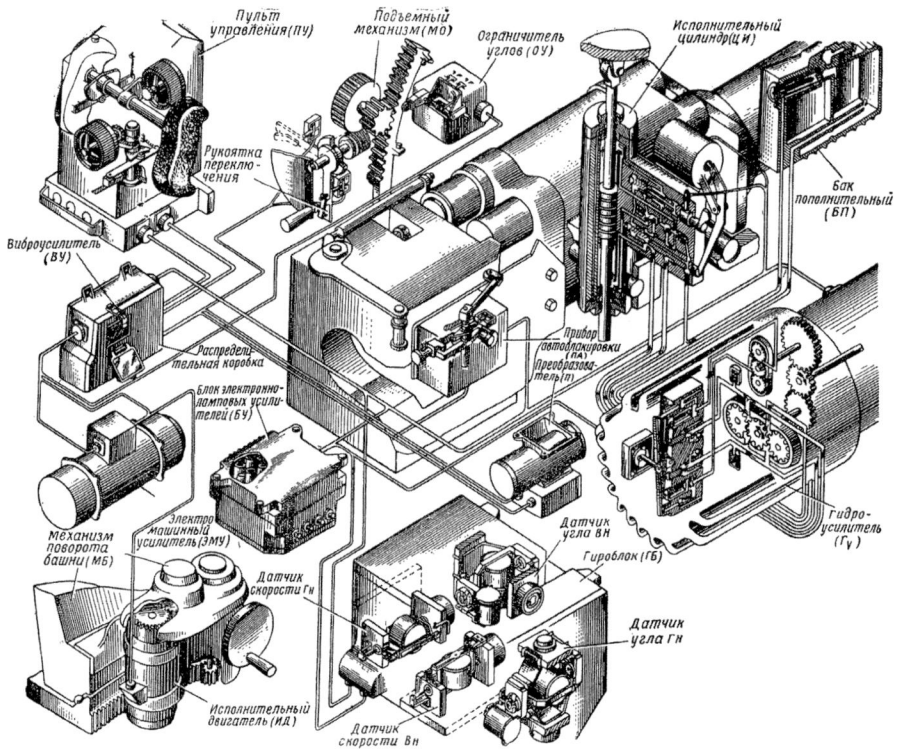

EXTENDING THE LIFESPAN OF THE T-55

The Soviet Army had a rather well thought-through standard for tanks and how to keep them operational. There were three standards for evaluation: technical inspection one (TO-1), technical inspection two (TO-2), and capital rebuilding. This was used for all tanks, with TO-1 taking place after about 2,500 kilometres or three years of operation, TO-2 at 5,000 kilometres or five years of operation, and capital rebuilding at 10,000 kilometres or ten years. Specific items such as tracks, clutches, fuel and water pumps, radiators, electronics, engines and transmissions were to be inspected and replaced at each of these intervals. Special 'Remontny Zavod' or 'Remzavod' rebuilding plants were set up to handle most of these operations, but on occasion the tanks would also be sent back to the production plants.

The potential battlefield environment also began to change during the first ten years of service life of the T-55 tank, by the end of which there were two new elements on the battlefield that had not been present when the tank was being designed. One of them was the introduction in large numbers of light armoured vehicles and personnel carriers such as the US M113, British FV432 and of course the Soviet BMP-1 and BTR-60. These lightly armoured vehicles included variants now being armed with first generation anti-tank guided missiles, making them a direct threat to tanks such as the T-55. But all of these lightly armoured vehicles were vulnerable to some degree to heavy machine guns such as the 12.7mm DShKM, which was still fitted to the T-54 series. The B-32 round could nominally penetrate 25mm of armour at close range, and later rounds like the BS with a tungsten carbide core could go even further. The 12.7mm DShKM turret weapon, deleted on the original T-55 design, now had a new role.

Also now entering the battlefield scenario and more relevant from a threat perspective was the advent of the attack helicopter armed with machine guns, cannon, rockets and ATGMs (anti-tank guided missiles). Slow flying compared to ground attack fighter-bombers, with speeds not faster than 320km/h, but carrying weapons deadly against tanks, these attack helicopters were, however, vulnerable to the 12.7mm AAMG fitted on the older Soviet tanks. Starting from 1969, the Soviets began to take measures to reinstall the AAMG mounts and weapons on T-55 and T-55A tanks, with 300 rounds in external stowage for the guns, while also fitting the same mount to the T-62 tank and other armoured vehicles such as the SU-85 (ASU-85) airborne self-propelled gun. All tank installations were generally referred to as the 'Model 1972' versions of these tanks. At least one Soviet rebuild plant appears to have also created a retrofit kit for the AAMG cupola and mount,

Syrian Arab Army (SAR) T-55 M-1969 during the Civil War
In Lebanon, Beirut, August 1976. It wears typical Syrian Army
three-colour camouflage. (Andrey Aksenov)

First T-55AM captured intact from the Georgian Army during fighting
around Abkhazian capital Sukhumi during the Civil War In Georgia, 1993.
New numbers as well as Abkhazian flags were applied above Georgian
markings on turret additional armour. (Andrey Aksenov)

as these were subsequently seen on tanks in Iraq and in service with other
foreign customers.

In 1977 a programme was undertaken to bring some of the T-54 tanks up
to the standard of the T-55, and as such a major programme was carried out

under the designator T-54M. This designator had also been used for an earlier proposed but stillborn upgrade to the T-54 in the mid 1950s and should not be confused with that programme. Full modernization called for the following:

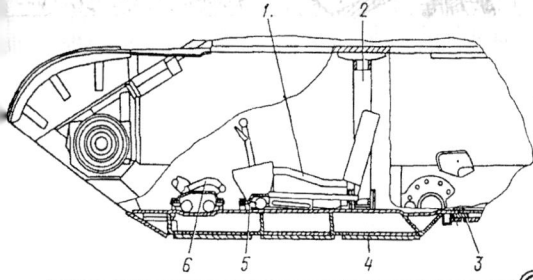

RIGHT A drawing of a T-55M fitted with the BDD armour upgrade package that started in the mid 1980s.
ABOVE The spaced armour protection provided by the BDD package for the lower front floor of the tank, providing mine protection to the driver-mechanic. His seat was also attached to the pillar (2) to avoid the direct transmission of shock to his body.

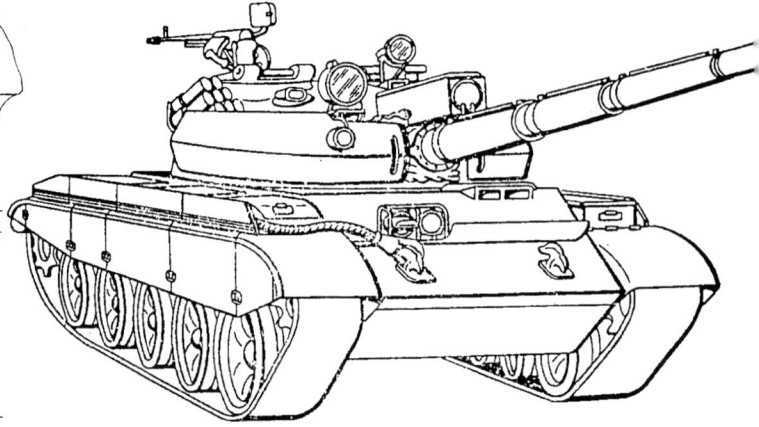

- Replacement of the D-10T gun with a D-10T2S and the 'Tsiklon' twin-axis gun stabilizer;
- Replacement of the SGMT machine guns with new PKT models;
- Installation of the TSh-32PM gunner's telescopic sight;
- Installation of the complete IR night fighting suite;
- Replacement of the V-54 engine with the V-55V of 580hp;
- Installation of the T-55 PAZ, PPO and TDA systems;
- Fitting of at least an R-123 radio set.

There were also T-54MK tanks built using the R-112 HF AM radio and antenna suite as well as a TNA-4 navigation system and independent generator set to provide power for the additional electrical load.

By the 1980s the T-55, which had entered service in 1958, was past its prime in its current configuration and was not tenable on modern battlefields as it stood. Combat evaluation from various battlefields where customers had used the tank showed several serious problems, of which the major ones were these:

- Vulnerability to RPG (rocket-propelled grenade), ATGM and HEAT (high-explosive anti-tank) ammunition. All of these could easily penetrate even the glacis and turret front of the tank, knocking it out and killing the crew.
- Vulnerability to mine damage. Not only would an anti-tank mine blow off a track or penetrate the hull, but just the shockwave of its detonation would invariably kill or cripple the driver-mechanic. This was due to his seat being firmly attached to the hull floor of the tank, so the shockwave was directly transmitted to his body.

- Limited effective gunnery range. The determined effective range of a T-55 armed with the 100mm D-10T2S gun was around 1,550–1,650 metres: that was the point where the tank had a 50 per cent chance of hitting its target and three tanks had a 50 per cent chance of destroying the target. But modern Western tanks had effective ranges out to 2,500–3,000 metres with laser rangefinders and fire control computers, and given suitable open ground could pick off the T-55 before they were within firing range. The same applied to anti-tank missile teams, who could outrange the tanks.

A suitable package was designed and developed to fit to both the T-55 and T-62 series tanks. The new equipment and fittings for the T-55, developed as the Obiekt-639 (production T-55M) and Obiekt-639AM (production T-55AM), included the following:

- An upgraded engine, first to the V-55U (developing 640hp) and later the V-46-5M (developing 690hp);
- The new 'Volna' fire control system with the 1K13 gunner's sight, KTD-2 laser rangefinder, BV-55 fire control computer, TShSM-32PV gunner's sight, 'Tsiklon-M1' stabilizer, missile laser guidance system, 9K116 'Bastion' bore-launched ATGM, a 9S831 power converter, and new controls and electronics;
- A spaced armour plate on the tank hull floor to protect against mine detonations under the forward part of the hull;
- Passive armour arrays consisting of stacked, thin spaced armour plates with surrounding resin filler on the glacis and frontal sides of the turret (these were colloquially nicknamed 'Il'yich's Eyebrows' in service after those features of Premier Leonid Brezhnev);
- Steel-reinforced rubber side skirts, providing a degree of protection against cumulative rounds;
- A suspended driver-mechanic's seat attached to the inside of the hull roof to protect the driver-mechanic from mine shockwave injuries;
- A set of eight Type 902B smoke grenade launchers from the 'Tucha' family;
- Increased dynamic travel to the suspension;
- Replacement of the older OMSh steel tracks with RMSh rubber-bushed steel tracks;
- Replacement of the R-113 or R-123 radio sets with the R-173 semi-solid state VHF FM transceiver.

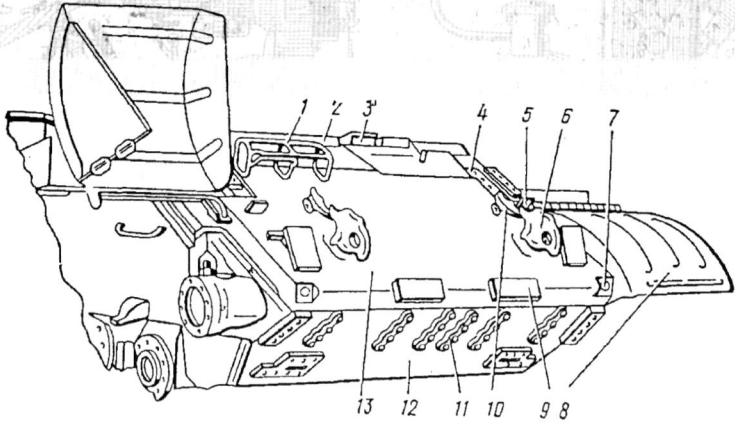

The bow of the BDD fitted tanks, showing the new upper glacis appliqué and how they moved components for the engineer equipment fittings around on the bow.

The 100mm 3UKB10-1 'Bastion' anti-tank guided missile in its transport arrangement fitted to a 100mm shell casing.

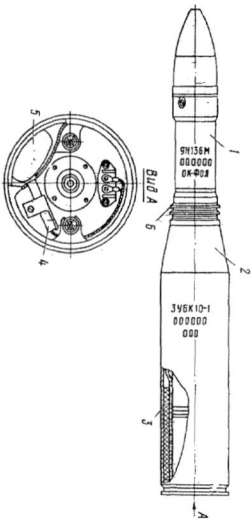

The new tanks were accepted for service in April 1983 under the following designators: T-55M (V-55U engine); T-55M-1 (V-46-5M engine); T-55M1 (without the 9K116 system); T-55M1-1 (without the 9K115 but with the V-46-5M engine); T-55AM (V-55U engine); T-55AM-1 (V-46-5M engine); T-55AM1 (without the 9K116 system); T-55AM1-1 (without the 9K116 system but with the V-46-5M engine).

Two years later, some of the tanks had their passive armour arrays on the glacis and turret removed and replaced with Dynamicheskaya Zaschita (DZ) or dynamic protection, known in the West as explosive reactive armour (ERA) for protection from enhanced HEAT projectiles. Typically, 44 boxes were placed on the upper glacis, 12 on the lower glacis, around 40 on the turret, and up to 84 on the side skirts. These tanks were designated either T-55MV or T-55AMV in service depending on the T-55 base model.

The upgrade permitted the Soviets to consider the improved T-55s to be 'main battle tanks' that could now fight against similar Western tanks (M60A3, Leopard 1Ax, AMX-30, Chieftain) on a relatively even level. The 'Bastion' bore-launched ATGM had a range of 4,000 metres and now provided the tank with the ability to effectively engage most threats as far as the crew had visibility.

MACHINE GUN ARMAMENT FOR THE T-55

As previously noted, the main identifying feature of the early T-55 and T-55A tank was their lack of the 12.7mm DShKM AAMG mount over the loader's hatch. But there were also other minor differences; for instance, the A models lacked a bow-mounted machine gun due to NBC sealing of the fighting compartment, as did the K or command models. The weapon was also deleted when the glacis was covered by either passive or explosive reactive armour additional protection.

(1) A T-55 with the post-1969 upgrades, which was located at Camp Greyling, Michigan, USA, in 1984. This tank appears to have undergone capital rebuilding in 1979 from data plates inside the tank and was provided to the Syrians. It was captured by the Israeli Defence Force in 1982 in Lebanon and then given to the US Army.

(2) This tank was in rough condition, but basically intact as provided. It still has the older RMSh tracks and 13-tooth type drive sprocket in place.

(3) All of the rear fittings, such as the auxiliary fuel tank brackets, unditching log and snorkel, were missing as it was delivered to the US.

(4) The tank also still has the small idler wheels, but does have the larger road wheel bearings on wheel station one.

(5) The rubber rims/tyres on some of the road wheels were 'chunked', but this may have been due to combat damage.

(6) This is a later production tank with the straight welded bow plate. It also has the later pressed steel splash board rather than the early wooden one.

(7) Most small details were missing, such as the marker lights. The linkage from the searchlight to the gun was also broken.

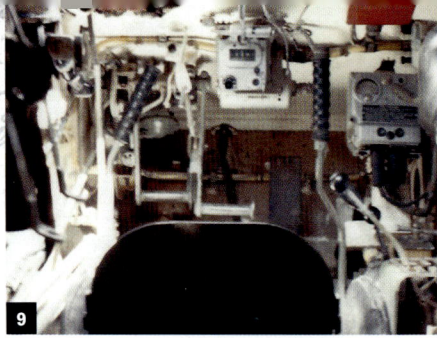

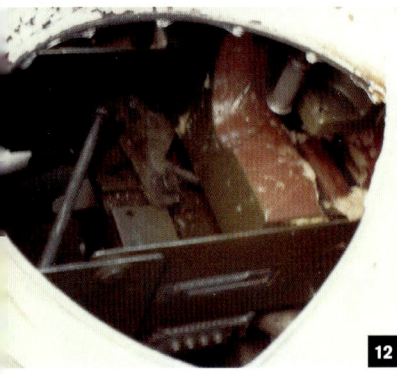

(8) The driver-mechanic's hatch was open and the vehicle was left accessible to the public.

(9) The driver-mechanic's position, with most of the major items still in place. The GKN-48 gyrocompass is in the centre of the photo, but the fixed bow gun to the right of the driver-mechanic has been removed. Also missing are the storage batteries.

(10) This is the driver-mechanic's main instrument panel on his right. Soviet tanks of this period had white interiors and grey floors, and fittings were in reddish plastic, olive drab, silver or grey, with some black motors and mechanisms.

(11) The twin 'stellazh' ammunition rack/fuel tanks and some other details are visible, including the rotating floor, ammunition clips on the right side of the hull, and the rack for the 250 round 7.62mm ammunition can for the co-axial machine gun.

(12) The breech of the 100mm D-10T2S gun. There are some broken parts of the tank located within the breech recoil guards.

(13) The exhaust has the pressed steel heat shroud in place, but this tank was not fitted with a set of mounts for the reserve oil tank, as seen on others.

(14) The rear radiator exhaust grilles on the tank, showing them to be higher in the front than the rear. The cover to the left is for fording purposes and seals the compartment, but leaves room for air to circulate from the fan.

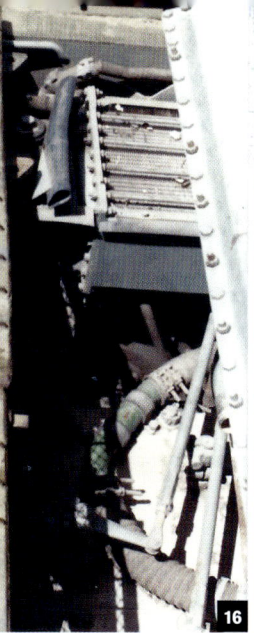

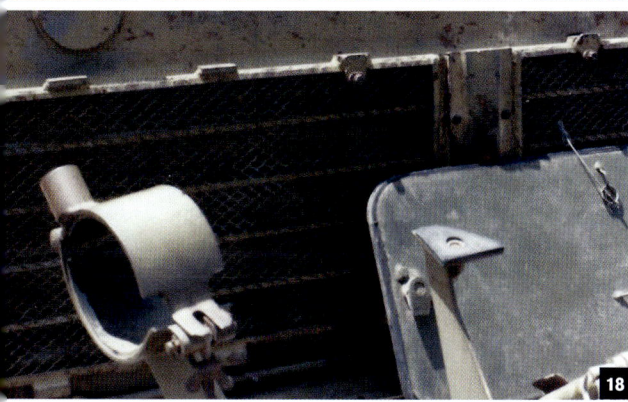

(15) Looking directly down into the engine compartment. The fan can be seen under the grille and two canisters for spare parts are located in the lower right rear of the compartment.

(16) On the other side of the compartment are three louvres, and in front of them (to the right) is the engine oil cooler.

(17) The V-55 engine, showing its fuel injection piping on the top of the manifold. Engine colours vary, and according to one source the colour of the engine indicates the manufacturing plant that rebuilt it; this one is painted in a soft grey-green colour.

(18) The top of the radiator intake assembly on the tank, which is fitted with an anti-debris mesh. Soviet designers well understood that tanks could suck in leaves, grass, fir needles and other debris, which would easily overheat the engines.

(19) The other side of the assembly, showing the main radiator. This is clipped to the deck for access to the transmission, but can be unclipped to work on that item. Note the filler nozzle at the upper right and the depression in the deck to clear it when the deck is closed.

(20) The oil pump stowage bin and the front right external fuel tank. All the fuel tanks were missing most of their filler caps.

(21)

(24)

(22)

(25)

(23)

(26)

(27)

(21) The rear fuel tanks, showing their connections to each other and the fuel system, as well as the cooling port for the 'guitara' transfer case.

(22) Unlike earlier T-55 models, these tanks were fitted with tie-down brackets in many places around the tank. The device in the centre is reportedly for filling and stacking ammunition belts for the machine guns.

(23) As noted, this tank was extensively damaged on receipt and the forward ZIP bin is proof of that. This tank is also missing the bin for the rammer and bore cleaning brush for the 100mm gun.

(24) The tanks fitted with the AAMG mount also had a set of transport brackets on the rear of the turret for use in administrative moves or temporary storage.

(25) On the right rear of the turret were brackets and guards to stow six 12.7mm 50-round ammunition cans outside the vehicle. The guards were to keep them from sliding out of their straps on rough ground.

(26) Squarely located in the centre of the rear of the turret are six tie-down brackets and a bar for mounting the storage tarpaulin when not in use.

(27) Unlike most of the T-54 AAMG mounts with the tourelle ring, the ones on the T-55 were welded in place, not bolted. They also had a different hatch.

(28) All T-55 turrets overhung the vertical sides of the hull, and as such a fillet was welded into place to match the turret race and associated turret diameter.

(29) The commander's cupola was left virtually unchanged.

(30) This OU-3 searchlight still has its rodding in place for operation, and the small wiper in front of the commander's sight is also visible.

(31) The loader's MK-4 viewer was missing on this tank. The AAMG mount for the 12.7mm DShKM machine gun also appears to have been knocked off in combat.

(32) The mount controls (elevation on the right handwheel, brake on the left handgrip for traverse) are still in place, but all of the rest is missing.

(33) The L-2 searchlight on this tank still has its rear cap in place.

(34) The bore evacuator of the 100mm D-10T2S gun in place. Barely visible are small notches on the muzzle for taping up string when bore-sighting the gun.

While all T-55s carried the 100mm D-10T2S gun, below is a summary table of the machine gun suites of the various tanks:

T-55 Model	Fixed Bow Gun 7.62mm	Co-axial Turret Gun 7.62mm	Anti-aircraft Gun 12.7mm
T-55 Model 1958	SGMT	SGMT	-
T-55K	-	SGMT	-
T-55A Model 1961	-	SGMT	-
T-55AK	-	SGMT	-
T-55 Model 1969	PKT	PKT	DShKM
T-55A Model 1969	-	PKT	DShKM
T-55M (all versions)	-	PKT	DShKM
T-55AM (all versions)	-	PKT	DShKM
T-55AD	PKT	PKT	DShKM
T-55MV	-	PKT	DShKM or NSVT 'Utes'/'Kord'
T-55AMV	-	PKT	DShKM or NSVT 'Utes'/'Kord'
Note: The 'Utes' and 'Kord' weapons are similar but are different machine guns in the same calibre.			

THE TWILIGHT YEARS IN SOVIET AND RUSSIAN SERVICE

As more and more new generation tanks appeared on the horizon, such as the American Abrams, the British Challenger 1 and 2, the German Leopard 2, and the French Le Clerc, the day of the T-55 was drawing to a close with the Soviet Army. When the Soviet Union collapsed in 1991, it was noted by General-Lieutenant Dmitry Vologonov that the USSR had a total of 77,000 combat tanks still on the books. He did admit that this figure included T-34-85, T-44M, IS-2M and IS-3M, and T-10 tanks in 'war reserve inventory' and located in depots throughout the country. But a good number of those tanks were T-54 and T-55 types in various stages of upgrading or deterioration based on where and when they had been last serviced.

Many of the tanks were distributed between the 15 new republics created by the dissolution of the Soviet Union. For example, in 1994 the Ukraine offered as many as 1,200 T-54 and T-55 tanks as scrap to Western countries, with Germany among other countries taking them for their very high-grade steels.

All of the upgrades and various changes over the protracted service life of the T-55 did come with a penalty, however. After the debacle of the Chechen invasion in December 1994, General-Lieutenant Sergey Maev (then head of GABTU, Gosudarstvennoye Avtomotivnoye Bronetankirovannoye Upravleniye – Main Automotive and Armoured Vehicle Directorate) noted that the Russian Army had dozens of different

РАБОЧЕЕ ПОЛОЖЕНИЕ
БОРТОВЫХ ЩИТКОВ

ПОЛОЖЕНИЕ
БОРТОВЫХ ЩИТКОВ
ПО-ПОХОДНОМУ

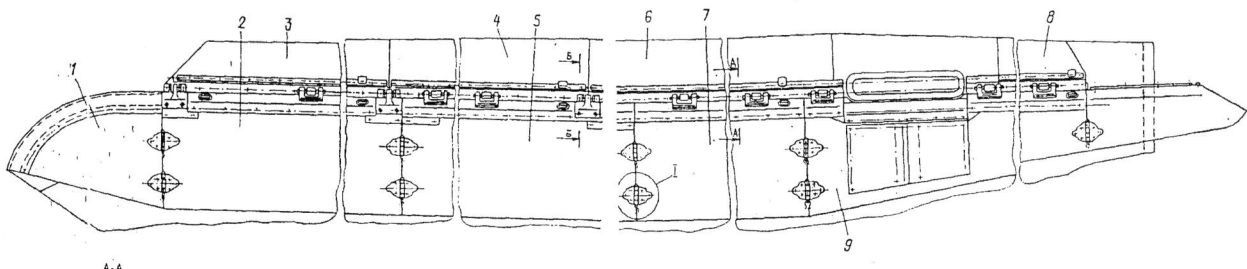

models of tanks in inventory, and many of them did not take the same parts or ammunition, which made operational maintenance difficult.

The Russian Federation sold off large numbers of these obsolescent tanks to client states, but the end finally came in 1997, when President Boris Yeltsin wrote off all surviving T-54 and T-55 tanks with the exception of a number of T-55AMV models. These latter tanks belonged to the Russian Naval Infantry and were kept for one basic reason: the load capacity of the 'Aist' class Landing Craft Air Cushion (LCAC) assault landing vessels. An 'Aist' could carry either one T-55AMV tank or 200 Naval Infantry troops; all of the other tanks in service with the post-Soviet Russian Army were at least six metric tonnes too heavy for deployment on the air cushion vessel.

A 1979 article in the Soviet military newspaper *Krasnaya Zvezda* stated that some 38,000 T-54 and T-55 tanks had been built when production ceased. Since there were 15,522 T-54 tanks of all models, it follows that from 1958 to 1979 around 23,000 T-55s of all types were built. Today the T-55 and T-55A still serve in the armies of many former Soviet and current Russian client states. Upgrades for these tanks are still offered by the Russian Federation and Western countries. Upgrades available include modification to the firepower, fire control, power plants, electronics and armour protection elements of the tank. With or without upgrades, T-55 tanks will continue to serve for many more years with many nations.

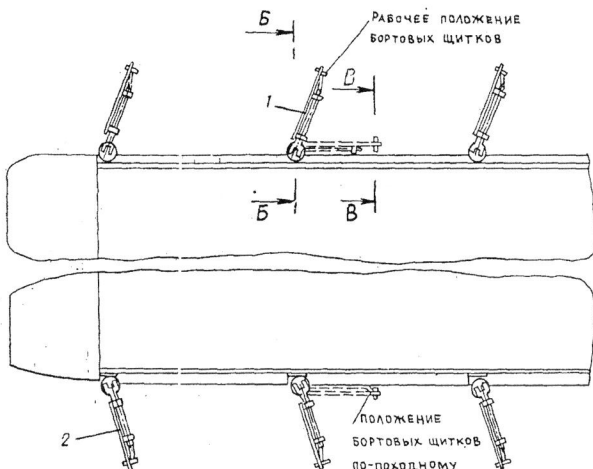

TOP The steel mesh reinforced rubber skirts fitted under the BDD program to the T-55 tanks as initially designed; later they would be fitted with either steel panels or 'Kontakt-1' explosive reactive armour modules.

ABOVE At one point the BDD armour fit also considered the use of the flap out 'gill'-type armour panels as used on the early model T-64 and T-72 tanks, but this apparently was not carried out on the T-55.

CHAPTER THREE

DESCRIPTION OF THE T-55 AND ITS VARIANTS

T-55 MODEL 1958 (OBIEKT-155)

Originally planned to be designated the T-54BM and given the Obiekt number 137G2M, the new tank was ultimately redesignated as the T-55 and given the Obiekt number 155. The tank underwent testing from October 1957 to March 1958, and after correcting some of the findings during testing it was accepted for service and full production on 24 May 1958.

As with the earlier T-54, the tank was divided into three distinct sections: control compartment, with the driver-mechanic seated on the left, with the storage batteries for the electrical system and the new combined fuel tank/rack for 20 rounds of ammunition on the right side; the fighting compartment, with the turret and more ammunition stowage; and the engine-transmission (MTO, Motorno-Transmissionaya Otdel') compartment, housing the engine, transfer case, transmission, planetary steering/final drives, radiator, oil cooler, transmission cooler, air cleaner, and fuel and oil tanks. The tank retained the rotating turret floor introduced in the T-54B. The internal volume of the tank under armour was slightly increased to 11.10m^3 compared with 10.52m^3 for the T-54.

The V-55 engine was another modification of the famous V-2. It now produced 580hp and was coupled to the same 5-speed transmission and 'guitara' transfer case arrangement as the earlier T-54. The running gear now used planetary steering for control versus the original band brakes fitted to the final drives and with a 13-tooth drive wheel using replaceable toothed disks; the band brakes now served as the main service brakes for the tank. Early production tanks retained the 810 x 165mm cast 'spider'* type wheels with 12 cast webs and lightening holes and the early T-54 type idler; the later five-spoke 'starfish' wheels were then used when inventory of the 'spider' wheel sets was exhausted, and would become the iconic T-55 wheel. The tracks remained the 580mm OMSh open metal-hinged tracks, which were good for at least 2,000 kilometres per set.

The suspension used four lever-type shock absorbers at road wheel stations 1 and 5 on each side of the hull, and primary

---

*   The terms 'spider' and 'starfish' are Western designations for ease of recognition, not original Soviet terms.

(1) A T-55 M-1958 being transported on a PMP pontoon bridge configured as a ferry during a Soviet Army exercise.

(2) A column of T-55A M-1958 tanks during a Soviet Army exercise in the Privolzhsky Military District in 1974. The lead tank has the straight glacis weld of the later T-55 but retains the central glacis machine gun port carried over from the T-54. (Y. Belozerov)

(3) A column of Soviet Army T-55 M-1958 tanks during a Soviet exercise.

(4) T-55 M-1958 tanks during a Soviet Army exercise. The original wheels on the second and fourth wheel stations have been replaced with older 'spiderweb' wheels associated with the early T-54, and earlier T-44 and T-34-85.

(5) A T-55 M-1958 fording a shallow river during a Soviet Army exercise.

(1) A T-55 Model 1958 at the T-34 Museum at Sholokhovo, near Moscow. This is a good example of the early production tank with no modifications.

(2) The museum has thoughtfully provided a platform for closer inspection of the tank.

(3) The tank is the standard production model, with the modified searchlight mounting connected to the gun barrel; early models had it welded to the mantlet.

(4) Most of the components are still in place on this tank, such as headlights and spare track links.

(5) The right side of the turret, showing the standard fittings such as the 'desant' handrails and the feed cable to the searchlight.

(6) Rear view, showing the hatch lock for storage. The rear cap of the searchlight is missing.

(7) Turret rear, showing the single lifting lug and the rear marker and identification lights. The latter is turned to the left; normally it has a mask with either slits or numbers pointing to the rear to identify the tank at night.

(8) Markings on the turret; 155 is the Obiekt (Object) number and 30 is probably the assembly group number, followed by a production serial for the turret casting.

(9) The loader's hatch showing its hold-open catch, lifting handle and locking assembly. The short strap is a welded-on device to prevent overzealous fans from opening the hatch!

(10) The commander's hatch with its spring-loaded flag and signal flare port visible. Note that this hatch too has a strap welded in place to prevent access.

(11) The left side of the commander's hatch. The viewer is missing in this shot, but the hole for the locking key is visible in the foreground.

(12) The driver-mechanic's hatch, showing the tubing that provides fluid to clean the two viewers during closed down driving.

(13) The L-2 main searchlight with the glass cover bolted in place. A separate metal cover is used to protect it from damage when not in use.

(14) The mantlet cover seal and rain guard at the top of the gun opening.

(15) Front view of the loader's hatch, showing the cover for the MK-4 view in place. The device can be traversed to provide differing views of the battlefield.

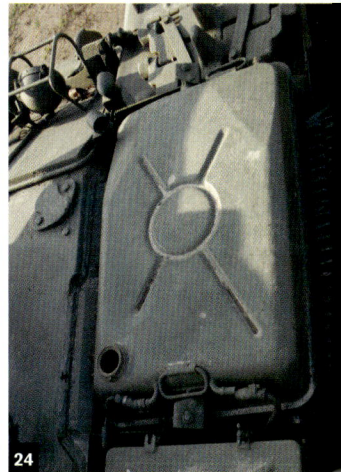

(16) Front view of the commander's hatch with the fixed MK-4 viewer for the gunner in the foreground. The OU-3 searchlight is missing but its control rod and cable access port are visible.

(17) Front view of the TVN sight head. This has an armoured cover that bolts to it when not in use, for protection.

(18) The long ZIP bin on the left fender is for a rammer and cleaning assembly for the 100mm gun.

(19) The method for fastening the exhaust to the hull is seen here.

(20) The method for mounting the reserve oil tank on the tank varied; this tank has it mounted on top of the exhaust heat shroud.

(21) The case at the rear of the left fender is for stowing the L-2 searchlight when not in use. The bulge is for the rear of the searchlight, which is stowed face down.

(22) The two rear external fuel tanks; someone has cut the outside connection hose between the two tanks.

(23) The stowage bin for the oil pump on the right fender.

(24) The front external fuel tank on the right fender. There are two spare track links forward of the tank.

(25) Normally this area of the right fender is used to stow the cover for the L-2 searchlight, but no brackets are installed.

(26) The right front corner of the hull roof. The two cover plates are for access to the fuel fillers for the 'stellazh' fuel tanks.

(27) Detailed shot, showing the front and side marker lights, the spring fitting for the front right mudguard, the headlight guard and the bracket for the splash board on the glacis.

(28) The marker lights point forward and at a 45° angle outboard and to the rear; they have a dull white light when turned on to give an idea of the tank's position at night. Rear ones are red.

(29) The headlight group, with the infrared light on the right and shrouded white light on the left. The horn was fitted here on some tanks, but normally was positioned under the left bulge of the turret race.

(30) The mantlet cover, showing its rod bracing and also the hinged connector rod from the gun to the searchlight platform.

(31) The engine deck, showing the radiator air intakes (bottom of photo) and the fan exhaust at the rear. Soviet tanks had square vents at the rear; Polish and Czech manufactured tanks had ones with an angular bulge to the front right.

(32) A T-55 Model 1958 in the collection of the Museum of the Ural Railway Wagon Plant (UVZ). The tank to the right is an Obiekt-167 prototype medium tank.

suspension was via torsion bars on all five road wheel stations. Stations 1 to 4 were trailing link and Station 5 was leading link; it retained this quirk from the T-54 series. There was a greater separation between the first and second road wheels on all of the T-54 and T-55 series tanks; this was due to the weight of the turret necessitating more support in the centre of the chassis. As production continued, later a larger and stronger hub assembly was used on road wheel station 1.

The tank retained the armour protection of the T-54B, with a 100mm upper glacis plate set at 60° from vertical and a 60mm lower one set at 45°. Side armour protection was 45mm set at zero and the rest of the hull armour was 10–15mm; the stern plate was 40mm at 0°. Frontal protection on the turret remained at 200–216mm.

As with the T-54B, the tank was fitted with the STP-2 'Tsiklon' twin-axis stabilizer. The 'Tsiklon' was essentially two different stabilizers working together to give a completely stabilized firing position for the 100mm gun. The system only required that the gunner hold his sight on the target; when the position of the gun matched the position of the crosshairs in the sight, the gun fired. This stabilizer was not supposed to be used for more than four hours to avoid overheating and damage. The gunner was also now given an azimuth indicator for the position of the turret.

The T-55 retained the TPKUB (after 1959 the TPKU-2) sight and vision device, and for night operation with the infrared system the commander had to replace it with a TKN-1 night sight. He also received a new OU-3 infrared searchlight for his cupola.

The driver-mechanic now received a new TVN-2 device and a second headlight, now infrared, was added to the basic equipment of the tank. The driver-mechanic would have to replace the clear headlight with the infrared one for use with his vision device. Starting from 1960, his seat also became adjustable in fore-and-aft travel.

The 100mm D-10T2S gun was initially provided with a TSh2B-22 telescopic sight for use with the gun and the co-axial 7.62mm SGMT machine gun to the right of the gun, with a second such weapon to the immediate right of the driver-mechanic in his control compartment. Total main gun ammunition was now 43 rounds and 3,500 rounds of 7.62mm. For use with his TPN-1-22-11 night sight, an L-2 infrared searchlight was located to the right and above the gun. Like the T-54B early models, it was mounted on a platform welded to the mantlet; later it would be moved to the right and fitted with linkage to the gun to permit it to elevate with the main gun barrel.

The T-55 was fitted with the OPVT-54B underwater driving system. This was to permit the tank to drive underwater to a depth of five metres and for no more than 700 metres, essentially to permit crossing the majority of rivers in Europe. The system consisted of fixed and attached components, most of which were permanently installed, such as seals for the occupied sections of the tank, an inflatable turret race seal, and mounts for a snorkel and exhaust flapper. There were rubber covers for the gun muzzle, telescopic sight port, and co-axial machine gun as well as various forms of folding covers and seals for the engine compartment. A four-metre-long snorkel attached to a small port on the commander's hatch and a one-way flapper device bolted to the flange fitted to the exhaust aperture on the left side of the hull. Initially the snorkels were of the two-section OPVT-54 type that consisted of two sections and were stowed at the rear of the hull; later a new design consisted of four nesting sections that were stowed on either the right front or left rear of the turret. Finally, four closed gas masks and life jackets were provided for crew escape if the tank stalled or flooded on the bottom of a river.

For underwater navigation the tank was provided with a GKN-48 gyrocompass; without it driver-mechanics in training were noted as wandering off course and in some cases running with the flow of a river rather than across it.

The tank retained the R-113 VHF FM radio set as well as the R-120 tank intercom system. The radio could use any of 1-, 3- or 4-metre whip antennae and gave a maximum range with voice communications of about 20 kilometres. The generator system of the vehicle was increased to 5kWt. The tank operated on a current of 24v DC power.

T-55K COMMAND TANK

As with the previous T-54 tank, the T-55 was also immediately followed into service by a command tank variant. The tank was proposed in January 1958 and was developed by Kartsev at Plant No. 183 (UVZ) in Nizhny Tagil. After testing from late 1958 to early 1959, the tank was approved for service on 3 September 1959 in accordance with Order No. 154 of the Soviet Ministry of Defence.

The T-55K was series produced from 1959 until July 1962 at Plant No. 183 (Nizhny Tagil), with approximately 200 T-55K tanks built there, and at Plant No. 174 (Omsk) from 1961 to 1963. In total 450 T-55K command tanks were built, as well as some at Kharkov.

The T-55K command tank retained the R-113 VHF FM radio set as well as the R-120 intercom system, but now added an R-112 HF AM radio set for

TOP T-55A tanks during a Soviet night firing exercise in the winter of 1964.
ABOVE A column of Soviet Army T-55A tanks crossing a river. The T-55A variant is readily distinguished by the sheet metal housing for the additional radiation lining.
LEFT Soviet Army T-55A tanks during manoeuvres. Note the turret stowage location of the OPVT snorkel.

command and control communications with other formations. The R-113 had a frequency range of 20–22MHz, but the R-112 had 220 fixed frequencies for tuning between 2800 and 4990KHz. The R-113 had a range of about 12–20 kilometres based on antenna used, but when using the R-112 with a 10-metre omnidirectional antenna and Morse code (at the halt as the vehicle could not move with this antenna erected), it could provide a communications range of 100 kilometres or more. Both radios used the same antenna and antenna mount on the move, and switching was done by the commander; this made battlefield detection of command tanks more difficult.

The T-55K command tank also had an AB-1/P-30 DC generator set for use at the halt with a supply of 15 litres carried for its use; this was located next to the driver-mechanic inside the fighting compartment.

The only major difference between the combat characteristics of the T-55 and the T-55K was that the latter only carried 38 main gun rounds. It also deleted the bow machine gun as the generator set occupied the same area and the area used for storing 7.62mm ammunition.

T-55A MEDIUM TANK (MODEL 1961) (OBIEKT-155A)

The T-55A was the result of a requirement for a more heavily protected tank for use in conditions of tactical nuclear warfare. It was specifically tasked to the Omsk design bureau within Plant No. 174 in Omsk for development, and as a result a new design bureau, OKB-174, was raised and headed by A. A. Morov (this later became the famous KBTM at Omsk).

The tank was able to use a great deal of material already developed and prototypes were prepared in the second half of 1961. By a Resolution of the Council of Ministers dated 20 February 1962, the tank was ordered into production, but it was not until 16 July 1962 that the tank was approved for service with the Soviet Army. This tank was primarily produced at Plant No. 75 in Kharkov and Plant No. 174 in Omsk.

The main difference between this tank and any other T-55 built during that time frame was the presence of the *podboy* anti-radiation liner inside the inhabited portions of the tank. Where it was not possible to easily install the liner, an appliqué (*nadboy*) was used such as on the outer surfaces of the crew hatches and around the sides of the commander's cupola, as well as a small area between the commander's and loader's hatches. The combat weight of the tank went up to 37.5 metric tonnes with the modifications and radiation shielding installed.

Due to the fitting of the liner and the necessity of sealing the hull, the bow machine gun and its ammunition were eliminated from these tanks.

T-55AK COMMAND TANK

As with the T-55, there was a command version of the T-55A tank. Also developed by OKB-174 in Omsk, design work was carried out per an order from the Ministry of Defence dated January 1963. Four prototypes underwent testing in the second half of 1963 under the original plant

(1) A T-55A Model 1961 at the Muzei Tekhniki (the Vadim Zadorozhny Museum) in Krasnogorsk near Moscow. This tank is relatively complete.

(2) This tank has the complete engineering equipment mount array fitted to the upper and lower glacis. However, the splash board is missing.

(3) Stowage differed very little between the Model 1958 and the Model 1961 tanks.

(4) This tank has the covers on the L-2 and OU-3 searchlights, a white light to the right of the searchlight, and the lenses still installed on its marker lights.

(5) The rear marker light and identification light are in place, but none of the tie-down brackets for the storage tarpaulin are installed on this tank.

(6) Conveniently, the identification light is fitted with stencils for tank number '55'!

(7) This tank is still fitted with the slotted brackets for the OPVT cover over the radiator area of the engine deck. Fuel tank mounts are fitted, but no brackets or tanks. The oil pump stowage bin is now at the rear of the left fender.

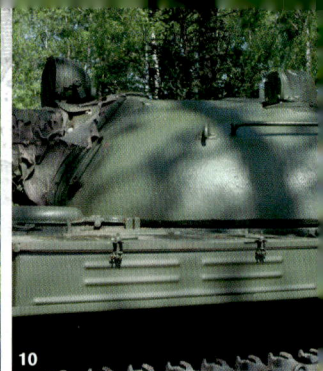

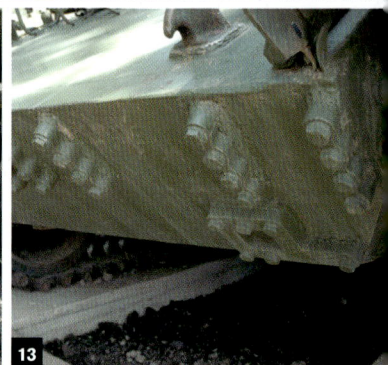

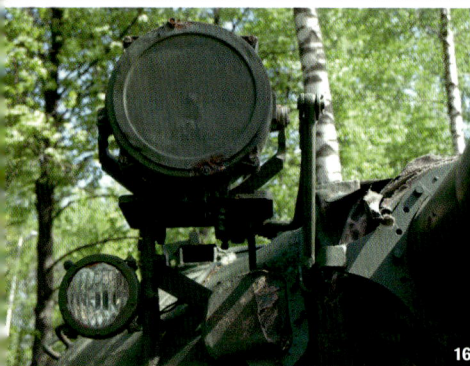

(8) This tank has rubber mudguards fitted to the ends of the fenders.

(9) The Model 1961 has its OU-3 searchlight fitted, but the infrared lens has been removed in lieu of the white light.

(10) Like the Model 1958, this tank is fitted with four 'desant' handrails, two on the left and two on the right.

(11) The left front fender of this tank carries the track locking mechanisms used to block the tracks on to a railway flat car for transport. They prevent the tank from moving once placed on the car and the clamps are locked in place.

(12) The Model 1961 has the definitive T-55 suspension, with the wider idler wheel at the front and the enlarged bearing of the station 1 road wheel set.

(13) A close-up of the engineering equipment fittings on the lower glacis. This tank has been retrofitted with the later OMSh tracks with rubber-buffered pins.

(14) The headlight assembly, a bit the worse for wear.

(15) The underside of the mantlet cover, showing more of the bracing rods. The object to the left is the wading cover for the machine gun, but with no gun in place it flops over.

(16) The L-2 searchlight, also minus its infrared lens cover, on its mount to the right of the gun. The white light headlight is fixed, but the main light is hinged and moves with the main gun.

(17) Due to the use of the *nadboy* radiation shielding, the viewers for the T-55A are slightly different in design than those of the T-55.

(18) The left side of the mantlet area, showing how the OPVT cover bracket for the telescopic sight stands proud of the turret.

(19) The hull rear, showing the brackets for the 200-litre auxiliary fuel tanks and the unditching log; the two-section snorkel brackets are located on the bottom of the fuel tank brackets and thus are missing.

(20) Two OMSh links carried on the right rear fender. The tank carries six spare links – two at the front, two at the rear, and two on the lower part of the stern plate.

(21) The two right rear external fuel tanks, showing the connections between the two tanks and also the piping to the tank's fuel system.

(22) The loader's hatch, showing the *podboy* appliqué and cover over the hatch; the hole is for access to the hatch lock.

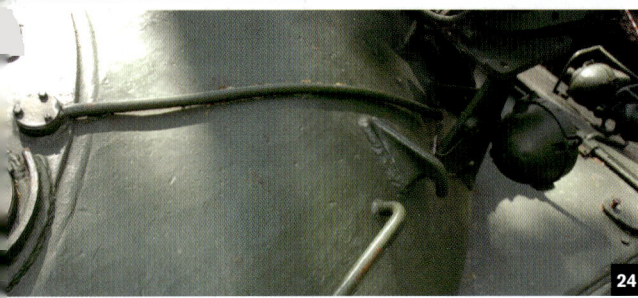

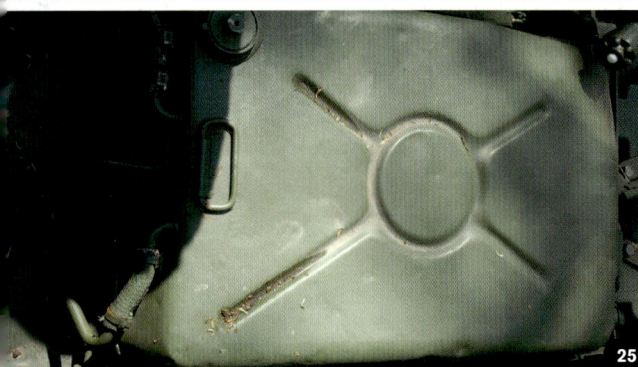

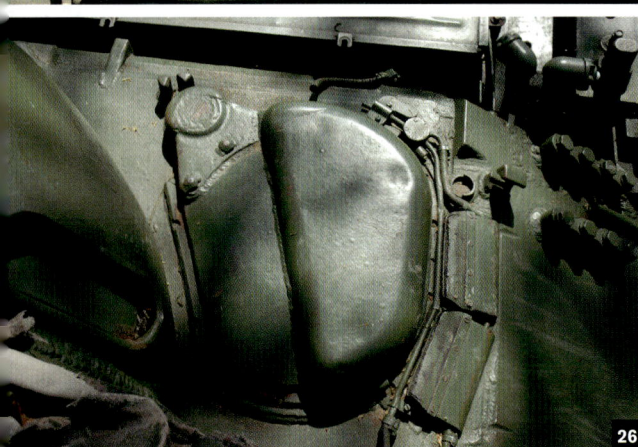

(23) The engine deck, with a clear view of the adjustable louvres inside the radiator air intakes and also those on the radiator exhaust grille at the upper right.

(24) The fitting with the power cable for the searchlight assembly at the front right of the turret.

(25) The front right external fuel tank and rearward-facing marker light assembly.

(26) The driver-mechanic's hatch showing the *podboy* shielding and cover over only half of the hatch, as well as the tubing for the viewer cleaning fluid.

(27) The commander's hatch area, showing how the *podboy* and *nadboy* anti-radiation shielding was applied to the vulnerable areas of the assembly.

(28) The turret roof, with a small section of *podboy* liner fitted between the commander's cupola and the loader's hatch.

(29) The rain guard part of the mantlet cover, which has unfortunately parted company with the fitting to the guard.

30 **31** **32**

33 **34**

35 **36**

(30) The MK-4 viewer provided for the loader. The small bracket to the front of the hatch may be for stowage of a device used to load machine gun belts.

(31) The fuel fittings for feeding the fuel from the external tanks into the tank's main fuel system. The small grille is for cooling air access to the 'guitara' transfer case.

(32) A view showing how the various covers over the shielding are attached to the turret.

(33) A view of the right rear fender with the rear marker light (also tail light) visible at the top of the photo.

(34) The left side of the tank, showing how the horn is fitted to the left turret race bulge.

(35) Most of the ZIP and stowage bins on Soviet tanks were fitted with handles so they could be easily removed when necessary.

(36) A view of the suspension, showing the new 14-tooth drive sprocket used with the OMSh tracks.

development designation of Obiekt-615, but it was accepted for service as Obiekt-155AK in accordance with Ministry of Defence Order No. 184 dated 24 June 1964 and given the service designator T-55AK. The tanks were built in small numbers only at Plant No. 174 in Omsk, with 24 built by the end of 1965, and with 150 of these tanks being built in total (still referred to internally at the manufacturing plant as Obiekt-615) before production ended in 1977.

Other than the fitting of the T-55A liners and appliqué to the tank, the T-55AK was identical to the T-55K with all of the same fittings and communications equipment.

T-55 'ALMAZ' FITTED WITH TANK TELEVISION EQUIPMENT

Based on a 4 November 1960 Resolution from the SM SSSR, VNII-100 in Leningrad carried out work on 'Topic 23' with the project name 'Almaz'. This was research to see if a television camera system could be fitted to tanks to improve driving and gunnery conditions when their optical devices were inoperative or could not determine either terrain or target conditions.

A standard T-55 tank was taken aside and refitted for this purpose. The forward fuel tank and 'stellazh' racks/fuel tanks were removed and four storage batteries moved into their original location. The commander/operator received an AZ-100 signal converter, an AZ-101 control panel, an AZ-117 automated control panel, a monitor, stabilizer and remote gunnery controls, and an observation and targeting camera position indicator. The driver-mechanic received an additional AZ-113 television camera and AZ-105 monitor. His camera port was mounted in the centre of the upper glacis in an armoured housing. Vision devices and sights on the turret were removed and replaced with two cameras in rotating mountings.

There were two channels on the television – observation and aiming. A switch permitted signals from any of the three cameras to be displayed on the monitors; commander and driver-mechanic had independent controls and input selectors. Stabilization was based on the 'Tsiklon' twin-axis armament stabilizer.

Testing at NIIBT Kubinka showed that the system worked well, but it was so large and bulky that it drastically lowered the overall combat capability of the tank (low ammunition capacity and no bow or co-axial machine guns as well as a reduction in range without the forward fuel tanks). Further development at that time was seen as not worthwhile.

(1) A T-55 at speed during a Soviet Army exercise. Note the additional fuel tank mounted above the standard configuration track guard mounted tanks.

(2) A rear view of a T-55 returning from a Red Square parade in the period 1962–64. Note the smoke canister and snorkel stowage configuration.

(3) A column of Soviet Army T-55 tanks on the move. The lead tank has the definitive straight glacis weld of the T-55, and no hull machine gun. Note the mask on the secondary searchlight below the L2 infrared searchlight for the main armament. These tanks are fitted with the original standard track. Note also the device on the gun muzzle.

(4) A T-55 exits a water obstacle with the TDA fuel injection system producing a covering smokescreen.

(5) A column of Soviet Army T-55 tanks on the march.

(6) A nice colour view of a Soviet Army T-55 during a manoeuvre, with 'desantniki' riding aboard the tank, a practice largely dropped post World War II. Note the D-10TG marking on the track guard pannier for the gun cleaning kit.

T-55 MEDIUM TANK WITH 'MALYUTKA' ATGM LAUNCHER (OBIEKT-614V)

As with all other Soviet tanks at the time, and also in compliance with the major push by Premier Nikita Khrushchev to turn to missile armaments in lieu of artillery weapons, in 1962 the T-55 was tested with a three-round launcher for the 9K11 ATGM firing the 9M14 'Malyutka' guided anti-tank rocket. The primary purpose of the additional turret-mounted ATGM was to allow tanks such as the T-54, T-55, the T-10 heavy tank and even the PT-76 amphibious light tank to engage enemy armour effectively to a range of 3,000 metres, well beyond the capability of the main armament fitted to these tanks.

The KB of Plant No. 174 in Omsk developed the system between 1961 and 1963 as the Obiekt-614A, a further development of the Obiekt-614 developed for the T-54. Testing was carried out with 15 prototypes converted by Plant No. 183 over the course of 1961 to 1963, with the same modifications being undertaken at Plant No. 174 with its T-55A tanks, which were designated Obiekt-625.

Each tank was fitted with a triple launcher mount in a 'cage' protective frame at the rear of the turret behind the loader's hatch. Immediately it was seen that the missiles were vulnerable to enemy fire, and due to sighting and aiming requirements they could not be fired on the move. The three missiles had to be carried inside the tank to prevent damage prior to combat and required five rounds of 100mm ammunition to be deleted to carry them in addition to the 9S429 missile controller.

The 9M14 missiles were sighted through a modified gunner's sight and were fired sequentially. Effective range was 500–4,000 metres. Their launcher was electronically operated and could elevate from -4° to +9° 45 minutes for launch.

T-55 M-1958 tanks undergoing capital repair at a TankoRemontny Zavod (TRZ) – Tank Repair Plant.

A modernised early T-55 M-1958 tank after capital rebuild.

It was decided that while the supplementary 9K11 ATGM system was workable, it was impractical for tanks to use this missile for several reasons. One was that the missiles were unprotected and vulnerable to shell fragments and small arms damage. Once fired, the crew then also had to get out and manually reload the 9M14 rockets, which was not practical in combat. Also the tank had to halt to fire them accurately and became more vulnerable. As a result, the programme was terminated.

INTERIM CHANGES AND IMPROVEMENTS

Unlike many other Soviet tanks, the T-55 and T-55A received incremental upgrades over the course of their production life in addition to capital rebuild improvements. The US Army would call these 'modification work orders' or MWOs, but the Soviet Army had no comparable plan, simply introducing improvements as they materialized. Morozov had seen exactly this problem during the war, hence his demand that he be given full control of the production of the T-34 to standardize improvements and to prevent this sort of variation in specific items on the tanks.

From the beginning the tank was designed to be fitted with the five-spoke cast 'starfish' wheels, but due to available supplies of the older 'spider' wheels some early production T-55s were fitted with those road wheels. Later on, a scalloped rim idler was introduced to provide more bearing surface for the tracks and prevent thrown tracks while traversing rough terrain.

(1) A T-55A with the AAMG position showing the post 1981 upgrades given to many T-55 tanks. This one is in the Great Patriotic War Military Museum in Kiev (Kyiv).

(2) Among other things, the tank now features OMSh tracks and the 14-tooth type drive sprocket.

(3) The tank retains all of the T-55A features, such as the radiation-shielded commander's cupola.

(4) A good close-up of the 14-tooth drive sprocket and rear of the tank with the revised oil pump stowage location.

(5)

(8)

(6)

(9)

(7)

(10)

(5) One of the new items fitted was the KTD-2 laser rangefinder and a BV-55 ballistic computer to integrate the data into the fire control system of the tank.

(6) This device has a small armoured door operated by the gunner which protects the rangefinder transmit and receive lenses.

(7) The tank is not, however, fitted with the 1K13 sight for use with the 'Bastion' missile system that was part of the definitive M series upgrades in 1985.

(8) The turret still shows the normal T-55 series features, such as 'desant' handrails and the cover over the telescopic sight port.

(9) The turret rear still carries the standard tie-down brackets and protective rails for mounting the storage tarpaulin, as well as the DShKM stowage brackets.

(10) The rear identification light is missing its mask and red lens.

In 1960 the dynamic travel of the torsion bar suspension was increased from 142mm to 162mm to improve the ability to cross uneven terrain. This also required resetting the maximum angle for flex of the bars from 48 to 53°. The torsion bars were given additional heat treatment.

About this time, work was also undertaken on the suspension components. The outcome was an increase in the diameter of the hub of the road wheels on Station 1, with a visually similar but larger design. Apparently too much wear was taking place on that wheel station during cross-country driving and a larger hub meant a longer life.

In 1962, meanwhile, the KB at Plant No. 174 developed and tested RMSh tracks for the T-55. The new design featured track pins encased in rubber so that track life was extended to 5,000–6,000 kilometres, while noise and vibration levels were reduced. The RMSh tracks were introduced on new build tanks from 1966, with older tanks being retrofitted as they underwent 'Capremont' or capital repair if needed.

In 1964 the FG-102 and FG-100 headlights were replaced by the FG-125 infrared light and the FG-127 blackout-shielded light for the driver-mechanic. The driver-mechanic could now use the FG-125 with his TVN-2 driver-mechanic's night periscope for night driving conditions; normally the FG-100 was in place and only replaced by the FG-125 when the infrared system was in use.

In 1966 the tanks began to be retrofitted or issued with the new R-123 VHF FM radio in place of the older R-113. The R-123 had a frequency range of 20–51.5MHz and offered a great deal more flexibility to the tank units, including the ability to contact infantry and artillery units in combat situations.

A number of the tanks were fitted with 12 mounts on the upper and lower glacis (four on the upper and eight on the lower) and two brackets for mounting either the BTU-55 bulldozer blade or a KMT-4 or KMT-5 wheeled mine trawl. All 12 of the rectangular mounts were secured with four large bolts in each one; the brackets were shaped something like an open soup pan and had more bolts along their perimeter. Depending on the device needed, they could be attached either by doubtless enthusiastic manual labour or with the help of engineers and a crane.

Most important and visible of all of the changes made to the tank was the reintroduction of the 12.7mm DShKM machine gun over the loader's hatch. By 1969 it was apparent that the new threat to Soviet armoured vehicles would be attack helicopters such as the AH-1 Huey Cobra and others in Western Europe. These were highly manoeuvrable but relatively slow targets (less than 320km/h top speed) and had to hover to fire ATGMs at tanks, so could be successfully engaged by anti-aircraft machine guns at ranges of 2,000 metres or less. There were also a lot of softer targets such as light armoured vehicles appearing on the battlefield that could be successfully engaged by a 12.7mm weapon with armour-piercing ammunition. The cupola was nearly identical to the older T-54 ones but had a new hatch design and some other changes, with only 300 rounds being provided for the weapon, all carried on the right rear outside of the turret. The T-55 (T-55A) with 12.7mm DShKM was formally introduced in 1972.

From 1974, some T-55 (T-55A) tanks were fitted with the KTD-1 laser rangefinder above the barrel. The KTD-1 was so fitted to T-55 (T-55A) tanks from 1975 to 1977. During the same time period, side skirts were added to some tanks.

Note that these incremental changes were applied to all T-55 models (T-55, T-55A, T-55K and T-55AK).

THE M SERIES UPGRADES (T-55M, T-55AM) (OBIEKT-155M/AM, OBIEKT-639M/AM)

By the 1980s the T-54 and T-55 tanks were seen as no longer able to stand in the frontal area as viable combat systems. They were now outranged by the armament and fire control systems on probable opposing tanks such as the US M60, British Chieftain and German Leopard 1 series, and the next generation M1 Abrams, Challenger 1 and Leopard 2 were even greater leaps ahead. But Soviet technology had a number of answers and it was felt that the T-55 in particular could be fully brought up to modern standards and turned into a main battle tank – the new emerging term used for tanks that carried out a variety of missions.

The first step was to increase the power needed for the tank, as all improvements would also increase the weight of the tank. As a result, a modified version of the T-55's V-55 engine, the V-55U, was introduced that produced 620hp. Alternatively a down-rated version of the T-72's V-46 engine could be used, the V-46-5M, which produced 690hp.

To go along with this, the torsion bars were replaced with a new design that was produced using an electroslag alloy. The new bars now provided a dynamic travel of up to 162–182mm. Finally, the tanks now received the RMSh tracks introduced in 1972 on the T-72 tank and a 14-tooth ring for the drive sprocket wheels to use with these new tracks. They were assessed as having a life span of 5,000 to 10,000 kilometres and provided a much quieter ride.

The tanks were given wider track guards with attached steel-reinforced rubber skirting like that used on the T-64/72/80 tanks of the period. These 10mm-thick panels provided some standoff protection against ATGMs and RPGs above the road wheels.

An original Soviet Army
T-55 M-1958 rebuilt to
T-55M standard. Note
the RMSh track and
combination armour
side skirts.

Old tanks never die – but they do get put out to pasture. Here a T-55AM2 with BDD armour package and an original T-55 sit in a storage depot to await their fate.

Mines, and a new threat – the improvised explosive device or IED – had shown themselves to be a serious problem in Afghanistan and the Middle East. The solution was to weld a vertical frame of armour plate to the bottom of the hull with attached horizontal plates 20mm thick to provide a standoff of about 80mm from the bottom of the hull. With the new torsion bars and dynamic travel, the tank only lost about 33mm of ground clearance with this new safety plate system. Also, the driver-mechanic was given a new seat, which was now suspended from the roof of the hull to reduce shock injuries.

The glacis and turret received upgrades to the BDD passive armour array system. They consisted of 30mm outer plates with staggered internal sets of thin 5mm-thick armoured panels spaced apart and then filled with an inert resin to give them more resistance. These added about 200mm of armour protection, primarily against HEAT projectiles, but also provided some protection against APDS and APFSDS rounds. Passive protection was completed with the 'Soda' anti-napalm fire reduction and suppression system.

Active protection was introduced in the form of a Type 902B eight-round 'Tucha' smoke grenade launcher system. This set of eight 76mm 3D6 smoke grenades could establish a one- to two-minute duration screen of up to 120 metres wide and 200–350 metres in front of the tank, using only four grenades.

Communications were changed out, with an R-173 semi-transistorized VHF FM radio set replacing R-113 and R-123 sets in most tanks as well as the new R-174 intercom system. This radio provided a frequency range of 30–79.90MHz, so again changed the options for communications. K model tanks received an R-134 HF AM transceiver to replace their old R-112 sets but retained most of the other equipment.

The primary part of the upgrade was, however, the new 'Volna' fire control system. This included the following components:

- A TShSM-32PV gunner's primary sight, now with an independent stabilizer in the vertical plane for the sight's field of view;
- An improved 'Tsiklon-M1' two-axis primary armament stabilizer;
- A thermal jacket for the 100mm D-10T2S gun barrel giving an improvement in accuracy of 5–10 times based on the weather and daytime conditions;
- The 9M116 guided armament complex, consisting of the 1K13 sight and guidance control providing laser guidance for an ATGM and the 3UBK10-1 projectile with the 9M117 100mm 'Bastion' through-the-tube launched ATGM;
- A 9S831 power converter for the system;
- A BV-55 ballistic computer for the D-10T2S to increase accuracy at long range;
- A KDT-1 (KTD-2) laser rangefinder mounted over the top of the mantlet (developed as the Obiekt-629).

The new system now provided the tank with a way to accurately range targets from 500 to 4,000 metres and engage them with the 9K117 'Bastion' missile. The missile used a HEAT warhead capable of penetrating up to 550mm of rolled homogeneous armour protection at any range.

The tanks received the following designators based on their variant and engine:

- T-55M – any T-55 with the full package and V-55U engine (Obiekt-155M);
- T-55M-1 – any T-55 with the full package and V-46-5M engine (Obiekt-155M1);
- T-55M1 – any T-55 minus the 'Bastion' system with V-55U engine (Obiekt-155M1);

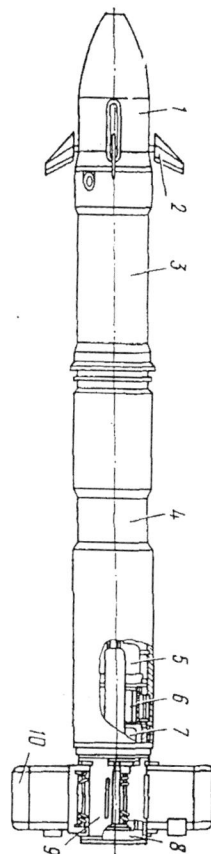

The 9M116 'Bastion' after firing/launch, with its guidance fins deployed as a guided missile.

- T-55M1-1 – any T-55 minus the 'Bastion' system with the V-46-5M engine;
- T-55AM – any T-55A with the full package and V-55U engine;
- T-55AM-1 – any T-55A with the full package and V-46-5M engine;
- T-55AM1 – any T-55A minus the 'Bastion' system with V-55U engine (Obiekt-155AM1);
- T-55AM1-1 – any T-55A minus the 'Bastion' system with V-46-5M engine (Obiekt-155AM1-1);
- T-55AM2 – export version of the T-55AM tank (also produced by Czech plants with their 'Kladivo' fire control system and a B suffix – T-55AM2B – and Poland, also with the 'Kladivo' system but with a different laser rangefinder and a P suffix – T-55AM2P) (Obiekt-155AM2).

Over the years, some of the tanks fitted with the DShKM mountings were upgraded from that weapon to either the 12.7mm NSVT 'Utes' or 6P7 'Kord' machine gun.

T-55AD 'DROZD' MEDIUM TANK (1983) (OBIEKT-155AD)

During World War II, armour designers had experimented with weaponry to defeat incoming projectiles, and starting in the 1950s the Soviets experimented with all sorts of ideas such as multi-barrelled 'Gatling'-type machine guns to shoot down incoming ATGMs. But that only worked against the very slow early NATO missiles such as the French-developed SS-10 and the American-designed Dart, and against faster and smaller missiles or RPG rounds they were essentially helpless. The systems were also quite bulky and towered above the tanks, as well as using an immense amount of ammunition to accomplish their task.

In 1964, the first elements of an active protection system were tested using T-55 tank hull sections as test pieces, which were fired upon by 85mm cumulative rounds for test purposes. Development of such active protection systems continued at a slow but steady pace for the next decade before the pace was increased in the late 1970s. Between 1977 and 1982 Soviet scientists worked on developing what they termed a complex for active defence (Kompleks Aktivno Zashchita or KAZ) to defeat new generation ATGMs and even RPGs. This bore fruit and on 12 September 1983 the Soviet Army adopted the Type 1030M 'Drozd' (Thrush) active protection system.

1

2

3

4

(1) A T-55AM2 upgrade tank in the Kubinka Tank Museum, showing all of the M upgrades with the BDD armour package.
(2) Components of the base tank were moved or rearranged to accept the new components, or, in the case of the splash board, replaced with a very short one.
(3) This tank has its three-section snorkel mounted on standoff brackets behind the left 'eyebrow' armour section.
(4) The three upper sections of the reinforced skirt protection are visible here.

(5) The two lugs on the outside of the 'eyebrow' section are for installation and mounting with a crane; they bolt on to the turret and can be replaced if damaged in combat.

(6) The auxiliary headlight (here an infrared lens one) was moved from the side of the searchlight mount to the front of the right 'eyebrow' armour section. The hull floor armour appliqué is just visible below the 'do not cross' rope.

(7) The 'eyebrow' armour provides protection for most of the frontal aspect of the turret and in the tank's frontal 60° arc, the most dangerous point of attack.

(8) In this view, the port cover for the 1K13 sight and missile tracker control is open.

(9) The hull floor armour appliqué is more visible in this photo of the Kubinka tank.

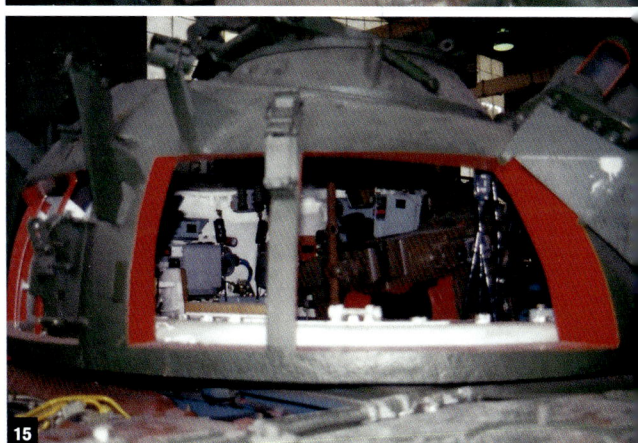

(10) A T-55AM2B tank from the former East German Army was at Camp Borden, Ontario, Canada, and as a trainer had been sectioned to show the interior and fittings of the M series upgrades. While it is a Czech built and upgraded T-55, the BDD armour package and other major details are the same as the Soviet version. Here the layered armour sheets surrounded with resin are visible inside the glacis armour package.

(11) The rear of the turret of the trainer, showing the thickness of the T-55's armour at the rear of the turret.

(12) The section of the front right aspect of the turret, showing the armour thickness as well as the outer end of the 'eyebrow' armour package, which is solid.

(13) The entire left side of the tank is cut open above the track run to show how components inside the hull are placed.

(14) Since this tank is a trainer, it has been fitted with external controls to operate parts of the tank for demonstration.

(15) The cutaway of the turret, showing the gun and major components inside the turret.

The 'Drozd' system consisted of three basic parts: a set of radar sensors on the front sides of the turret; a fire control computer dedicated to the system; and eight launcher tubes mounted in pairs and angled outward from the sides of the turret, each holding one 3UOF14 107mm anti-missile projectile loaded with what would be termed and well understood abroad as case shot.

The system operated in the following manner: when the radar on one or the other side of the tank picked up an incoming projectile 130 metres out, the system was activated and a launcher covering that sector was selected to engage the projectile. When the projectile closed to 60 metres, the radar would lock on and the computer prepared to fire. The munition was fired and detonated 6.7 metres in front of the tank, with the resulting detonation shredding the projectile like a giant shotgun.

The system was primarily mounted externally, with the radar elements at the top edge of the turret, the launcher tubes in splayed pairs welded to the side of the turret of the T-55, and the controller and computer in an armoured box on the rear of the turret. It only covered four different frontal sectors but the blast of the munitions was sufficient to cover a wide area. Scientists gave it a 70 per cent plus chance of properly engaging and destroying any incoming projectile travelling at 70 to 700 metres per second.

The tanks were fitted with blockers to prevent firing over the open hatch of the driver-mechanic and a normally redundant back-up generator was provided to ensure sufficient power would be available in an emergency to operate the system.

A portion of the T-55AD tanks were also upgraded with the M package as well as the T-55AMD, but the only change in designators was the T-55AD-1 (Obiekt-155AD-1) version, which was fitted with the V-46-5M in place of the V-55U.

All of this was scientifically well and good, and calculations were that the system would reduce battlefield tank losses by a factor of 2 to 3. But in all of the planning nobody asked the motorized rifle troops (who would be on the battlefield and in many cases in front of the tanks) their opinion. Commanders who were briefed on the system were absolutely indignant about putting their men out in front of something that could fire what was effectively a 107mm (approximately 4 inch) calibre shotgun at them without warning. It was admitted that the secondary use of the system was in manual mode to engage enemy troops at close range, which again did not endear it to the motorized rifle personnel.

While a considerable number of T-55A tanks were converted to T-55AD standards (over 700 were on paper still in Soviet inventory as of November 1990) it is not known how or if the General Staff determined how to use these vehicles operationally without injuring their own troops.

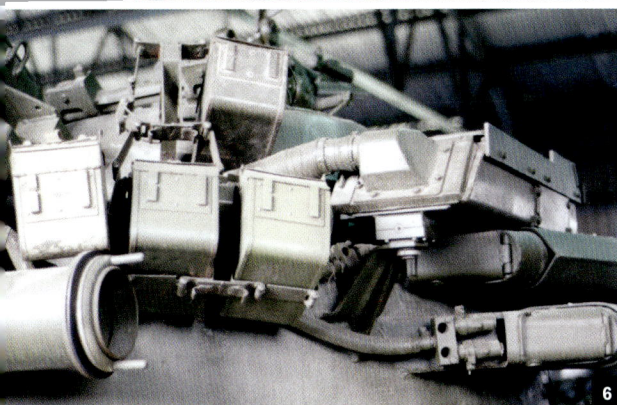

(1) The T-55AD fitted with the 'Drozd' (Thrush) anti-tank projective system, this one being at the Kubinka Scientific Test Range for Armour (NIIBT).

(2) This particular tank has seen several upgrades, such as the 1K13 ATGM launcher system and a set of Type 902B 'Tucha' smoke grenade launchers, as well as the 'Drozd' active defence package.

(3) Each side of the turret is fitted with four launchers for the rocket-propelled defensive munitions and their associated radar antennae on top of the twin two-round launchers.

(4) The computer that controls 'Drozd' is mounted at the rear of the turret; this tank also stows the three-section snorkel directly below the electronics chest.

(5) As the tank is fitted with the DShKM machine gun, the ammunition canisters need to be stored somewhere, and here four are wedged into the space between the launchers and the electronics chest. Two more are on the left side in a similar location.

(6) A close-up of the four 12.7mm canisters in place.

(7) The same tank during firing trials at the NIIBT polygon at Kubinka.

(8) The right front side of the tank. Many Soviet experts were not happy at the amount of controls and wiring now exposed on the outside of the turret, hence the system being vulnerable to damage from artillery.

(9) The snorkel has been unclipped from the tank here, showing the two clips that hold it in place on the rear of the turret.

(10) Another T-55AD within the Kubinka Tank Museum. Its machine gun has been removed from its mount.

(11) Although in somewhat rough condition, this tank has the steel mesh reinforced side skirts attached.

(12) Details of the radar over the right launcher assembly are visible, as are the insides of the tubes with no munitions loaded.

(13) The two brackets for the 12.7mm ammunition canisters are visible here on the left side.

(14) The left side of the Kubinka Tank Museum vehicle after some 'TLC' touch-up painting.

(15) The left side at an earlier date, showing the radar and launcher assembly.

(16) Rear section of skirting on the Kubinka Museum tank, showing the heat shield and drip protector for the exhaust.

(17) Another T-55AD 'Drozd' tank on display during the 'Armiya' exhibition in 2017.

Note that Poland also offered a T-55D tank, but it was a considerably different model, and essentially was a T-55 with a turret bulge to carry additional radio communications equipment for command and control.

THE T-55MV AND T-55AMV UPGRADES (1985)

At the same time that much of the M series development was going on, a parallel series of developments were taking place in regard to less dangerous active protection measures for tanks.

During World War II, German and Soviet scientists had also investigated measures to defeat infantry-operated shaped charge weapons such as the 'Panzerfaust' and 'Bazooka'. The measures essentially boiled down to having some sort of explosive charge disrupt the molten stream of metal created by the shaped charge warhead, thereby preventing it from touching the base armour of the vehicle. While the Germans did not succeed, Soviet scientists at the NII-48 institute did this in the late 1940s. But at that time no Soviet commander would accept strapping explosives on the outside of a tank and taking them into combat, so the project was shelved.

In 1964, two glacis armour sections from standard T-55 production tanks were submitted to firing trials against two variants of 'DZ' or dynamic protection, but the idea of such reactive armour did not progress further for almost another two decades, largely for the reason detailed above.

In 1982 the Israeli Defence Forces (IDF) went into Lebanon during Operation *Peace for Galilee*, and there the Syrians first encountered Israeli tanks fitted out with 'Blazer' reactive armour segments. These worked by having two plates of metal encase a small layer of explosives between them and then having the plates installed in a metal casing to protect them from the elements. When hit by a shaped charge projectile (ATGM, HEAT round or RPG) the explosive would detonate and the 'flyer' plates would totally disrupt the molten metal stream and reduce or negate its effect. The explosive was safe enough and the elements were protected from each other, so normally only one segment would detonate at a time. The only way to damage such vehicles was with multiple hits on the same spot, an unlikely prospect during a battle of manoeuvre.

The Soviet General Staff and Ground Forces were taken aback when the scientists showed them a captured M48 tank fitted with 'Blazer' additional armour, which negated all of their arguments. A crash project was begun at the NIIBT institute at Kubinka under V. N. Bryzgov to restart the Soviet indigenous reactive armour programme. This was approved (this time around) and started being deployed early in 1985 as the 'Kontakt-1' complex of dynamic protection

(1) A T-55AMV at the Stalin Line Museum in Belarus. While there are T-55MV variants, most tend to be based on the T-55A, either with or without the AAMG.

(2) While fitted with 'Kontakt-1' reactive armour, the tanks otherwise have the M equipment and also the standoff hull floor armour from the BDD armour package.

(3) The ERA bricks were fitted by depot level workshops, but in this case the two closest to the gun are probably not functional, as they cannot hold the two flyer plates used inside the weather cover ('brick').

(4) There are a number of options for mounting the ERA. This tank uses overlapping rather than wedge-shaped fittings.

(5) This tank has the later version of the laser range finder, with flip-down armour door in place of the other side-opening one.

(6) This tank also does not have the full ERA fit, as the rest of the bricks are mounted on the reinforced rubber skirts, which are not present here.

(7) The reactive armour is, like all appliqué fits, supposed to protect the frontal 60° arc of the tank; from what can be seen here, this one is a bit dubious in providing that protection.

(8) While this is a later model tank with the straight weld glacis, many others have ERA fits all the way to the edge, which this one does not.

(9) There is a considerable gap between the protection and the gun, mostly due to the need to provide for movement of the machine gun, which leaves the tank vulnerable.

(10) Given that the wedge-shaped bricks are supposed to be used on the top of an ERA fitting due to probable impact angles, this set-up may have been for museum display purposes only.

(11) Other than the frontal 60° arc, there is no other protection for the turret.

(12) Likewise, the left side fit is not properly installed. However, since most tanks do not have the ERA flyer plates fitted until readying for combat, this could be resolved later.

(13) Objects like headlights cause problems when fitting ERA to the glacis. In this case they seem to have fitted it in spite of the headlights!

(14) A Ukrainian T-55AMV with a full ERA fit based on manufacturing plant layouts rather than field ones. This tank has a much better protection suite than the tank located at the Stalin Line museum.

(15) This is a later model T-55A, with the AAMG, and shows its eight-round Type 902B 'Tucha' cluster behind the ERA fit.

(16) Note that both the glacis and turret have upper and lower sets of ERA fitted to protect the tank over a larger area of its 60° frontal arc, as well as the side skirt fit.

(17) T-55AMV tanks within a capital rebuilding facility (TRZ). All of these tanks have been fitted with their hull and turret ERA fit-outs and are awaiting a new set of OMSh tracks.

(18) Just visible in the bottom of this photo is the BDD hull floor pan armour assembly.

(19) Completed tanks with their tracks and skirts fitted and turrets reversed.

(20) The three-section snorkel is mounted in the same fashion as with the BDD fitted tanks.

(21) Another view of the tanks awaiting their tracks and side skirts.

(22) Yet another glacis ERA fit, this time on a VMF Naval Infantry tank seen during an open day.

(23) Like the Ukrainian tanks, this tank has a much better arrangement of its turret ERA, with extra bricks protecting the area next to the gun.

(24) This tank appears to have two tarpaulins installed, one under the snorkel and one in the usual location at the rear of the turret.

(25) The tank has a complete side skirt fit of ERA, but uses blocks four high rather than the more common three high, with the fourth brick attached to the above-the-fender skirting.

(26) A head-on view. This tank also has the driver-mechanic's foul weather hood in place, probably for use when making landings from Aist-class LCAC vessels.

(Kompleks Dinamicheskoy Zashchita or KDZ) with its elements of dynamic protection (Ehlementy DinamicheskoyZzashchita or EhDZ) fitted to first the T-80B and T-64B tanks and then to other tanks down the line.

The T-55M and T-55AM tanks were also fitted out with sets of EhDZ. A full set could include 12 elements (designated 'bricks' in the West due to their shape) on the lower glacis, 44 on the upper glacis, up to 42 on each skirt section, 21 on the left front of the turret, and 16 on the right side (the searchlight mount blocked a place to put some of the 'bricks') for a maximum total of around 177 'bricks' on the tank. During peacetime the 'bricks' were mounted, but without any of the 'flyer' plates installed for both safety and to prevent damage.

The tanks were correspondingly called the T-55MV (Obiekt-155MV) and T-55AMV (Obiekt-155AMV) with the V indicating *vzryvatel'nyy* or explosive armour. There were also T-55MV-1 (Obiekt-155MV-1) and T-55AMV-1 (Obiekt-155AMV-1) tanks to designate those upgraded with the V-46-5M engine.

One problem the Russians later had in Chechnya was that the first tanks sent in to the semi-autonomous republic in December 1994 did not have the 'flyer' plates loaded, as crews were inexperienced and commanders were not ordered to carry out those operations prior to operational deployment. Initially it was reported that 'Kontakt-1' was a failure until it was realized what had not been done. Since then it has performed as advertised on a number of different tank types, and where used on the T-55 tanks has also provided good results under most circumstances.

The Russians were, however, aware that 'Kontakt-1' was not effective against APDSFS ammunition as the plates were not strong enough to deflect or shatter the penetrators. A second version, the so-called 'Generation 1.5' EhDZ called 'Kontakt-5', does have some capability in this area. It is interchangeable with the fittings for 'Kontakt-1' and therefore it is not possible to tell which one is fitted. It is likely that this was retrofitted to the surviving T-55MV and T-55AMV tanks used by Russian naval infantry.

As of November 1990 there were at least 400 of these tanks remaining in Soviet service, but those numbers have been reduced to only a few operational battalions today.

THE OMSK KBTM T-55 'SWANSONG MODEL' UPGRADES

In the late 1990s, the KBTM design bureau in Omsk (Konstruktorskoye Byuro Transportnogo Mashinostroenya, Design Bureau for Transport Vehicles, also known as OKBTM) developed two potential major upgrade versions of the venerable T-55. The developments were undertaken at a time when funding was tight and contracts from the Russian Ministry of Defence were limited. The tanks were developed as other options to modernize the T-55, as an alternative to new tanks such as the then-concurrent and highly secret Obiekt-640 'Chorny Oryel' (Black Eagle) new MBT. The designs were developed in competition, providing alternative upgrades of the well-proven and reliable T-55 tank, the earliest of which were already nearly 40 years in service, for the Russian Army and as upgrades for export clients worldwide. The revisiting and upgrading of proven and long-serving tanks as an alternative to high-risk and high-cost new developments has recently been repeated with the introduction of the T-72BM3 MBT as a general service alternative to the high technology and thereby high cost T-14 'Armata' MBT.

T-55M5 (OBIEKT-155M5)

The T-55M5 modernization of the T-55 MBT included the following upgrades:

- New fire control system;
- New TKN-1SM sight for the commander;
- Thermally insulated main armament;
- 12.7mm NSV AAMG installation;
- Built-in DZ for the hull and turret;
- Side skirts with protection against cumulative rounds;
- New smoke grenade launcher assemblies;
- New fire protection system;
- New absorbent paint;
- New TVK-3 vision device for the driver-mechanic;
- V-55U engine with increased power output;
- Improved radio communications.

T-55M6 (OBIEKT-155M6)

The T-55M6 was an altogether more radical redesign of the original T-55, with new 125mm armament, a lengthened chassis with an additional road wheel pair, and the crew reduced to three personnel.

The T-55M6 modernization of the T-55 MBT included the following upgrades:

- 125mm smoothbore 2A46M series tank gun with autoloader and 22 round cassette;

TOP LEFT Starting from 1999, KBTM in Omsk began development of two new T-55 variants, the T-55M5 and T-55M6. The T-55M5 was a fully upgraded T-55AM while the more radical T-55M6 now mounted a 125mm 2A46M series gun and autoloader. This is the T-55M5 version. (Andrey Aksenov)

TOP RIGHT The T-55M5 has a complete fit of 'Kontakt-5' second generation reactive armour that is also partially effective against APFSDS ammunition, which 'Kontakt-1' was not. (Andrey Aksenov)

ABOVE LEFT The tank has multiple flyer plates in each module of protection and can take more than one hit on a module. (Andrey Aksenov)

ABOVE RIGHT Also note the tank has been fitted with either an NSVT or 'Kord' 12.7mm machine gun in place of the older DShKM weapon. (Andrey Aksenov)

LEFT The 'Kontakt-5' modules are better designed to protect the turret and cover more than most of the 'Kontakt-1' fits did. (Andrey Aksenov)

(Image series continues overleaf)

TOP LEFT The three-section snorkel is in the same position at the rear of the turret. Also note the machine gun belt filling device is now located underneath the snorkel. (Andrey Aksenov)

TOP RIGHT The tank now seems only to have three plus one 12.7mm ammunition canisters for only 200 total ready rounds. (Andrey Aksenov)

ABOVE LEFT The turret 'Kontakt-5' modules are paired with upper and lower sections, with the lower one overlapping the upper. (Andrey Aksenov)

ABOVE MIDDLE The tank also now features the later T-72 road wheels versus the older 'starfish' wheels used on T-55s since 1958. (Andrey Aksenov)

ABOVE The prototypes were shown in 2001 and subsequent years at the VTTV exhibtions in Omsk, but neither tank model progressed beyond prototype stage. (Andrey Aksenov)

LEFT The T-55 M5 during trials at the military polygon in Omsk. (Andrey Aksenov)

- Crew reduced to three by use of an autoloader for the main armament;
- 9K120 or 9K119 guided rocket options;
- 1A40-1 or 1A42 fire control systems (from the T-72B and T-80U respectively);
- RMSh track;
- Combination built-in and additional armour to the level of the T-80U;
- Grenade launchers;

TOP The T-55M6 variant was far more radical than the T-55M5, as it featured an extended hull with a new suspension layout as well as the 125mm 2A46M gun and the accompanying 'Zhelud' 22-round cassette-type autoloader. (Andrey Aksenov)

CENTRE LEFT KTBM made good use of available components to produce new variations on older tanks, and this tank is no different. It now features six road wheels as well as new side skirts and other hull modifications. (Andrey Aksenov)

CENTRE RIGHT The T-55 turret has now been swapped out completely for the T-72B style turret, humorously defined by Western intelligence as the 'Super Dolly Parton' for its extensive frontal lobe bulges. (Andrey Aksenov)

LEFT The T-55M6 also features T-80-style side skirts with armoured panels at the front. (Andrey Aksenov)

BOTTOM The tank is fitted with a 690hp engine, but does not have the 'sil'fon' thermal suppression exhaust system fitted to late model T-90 and upgraded T-72 tanks. (Andrey Aksenov)

TOP LEFT The side skirts have been extended to provide more coverage of the suspension. (Andrey Aksenov)

TOP RIGHT Another bustle extension similar to those fitted to the Obiekt-640/641 'Cherny Oryol' (Black Eagle) tanks is fitted to this turret, but as with those tanks Omsk has covered it with camouflage netting to hide details. The three-section snorkel is visible under the netting on the back panel. (Andrey Aksenov)

ABOVE LEFT The tank shows the hallmark KBTM use of available parts. From front to rear: T-80 road wheel (station 1); T-72 road wheel (station 2); T-55 road wheels (stations 3 and 4); and T-72 road wheels (stations 5 and 6). (Andrey Aksenov)

CENTRE RIGHT The turret shows its T-72 origins, but from the driver-mechanic's hatch the rest of the tank shows it began as a T-55A. (Andrey Aksenov)

CENTRE RIGHT Also on this side – road wheel station 1 is a T-80, but the other five are from a T-72. It appears that a new bow and glacis from another tank, perhaps a T-72, were grafted onto a T-55 hull to make this conversion. (Andrey Aksenov)

BOTTOM RIGHT From the wheel spacing seen here – with a standard T-55 configuration for road wheels 2 through 6 – the grafted bow section seems to be where the extra road wheels came from when applied to this tank. (Andrey Aksenov)

- Diesel engine uprated to 690hp;
- Maximum road speed: 50km/h;
- Maximum range: 500 kilometres.

Neither prototype was accepted for service with the Russian Army, and the alternative upgrade projects were filed when OKBM was merged with UVZ in Nizhny Tagil.

HOW MANY T-55 TANKS WERE ACTUALLY BUILT?

At the present time, the answer to this seemingly straightforward question is that there are no good records outside of Soviet (now Russian) state archives that completely answer that question.

Accurate totals are available through 1965 and show that the three Soviet production plants had built a total of 8,925 T-55s of all types and 1,505 T-55A type tanks by the end of that year. Between 1962 and 1979, 4,435 T-55A tanks and 150 T-55AK tanks were built by Kharkov and Omsk combined. Varying sources give the final Soviet-built totals as over 20,000; over 23,000; over 33,000; or, including the Polish- and Czechoslovakian-built tanks, over 68,000.

The Czechoslovakian Republic (CSSR) built 8,300 T-55 tanks, and Poland built another 7,000 T-55s on its own. While some sources also include Chinese Type 69 series tanks as well, these tanks, while having most of the same combat capabilities as the T-55, are not really T-55-based tanks and should not be included.

A large number of T-55-based chassis were also built, mostly by Omsk or at the STZ Martin plant in the Czechoslovakian SSR. That also adds another 7,705 known chassis to the mix.

Based on the 1979 *Kraznaya Zvedza* article indicating 23,000 plus T-55s of all types were built in the USSR, this would give a total of all T-55s including the Czech and Polish models of around 38,000. Today more than 32,000 T-54s and T-55s remain in service with some 40 user nations, which is testimony to the strength and endurance of the original design.

CHAPTER FOUR
DERIVATIVES OF THE T-55 TANK FAMILY

The T-54 tank had been built in very large numbers, with a number of series production variants and prototype developments built on the chassis over the years. The T-55 was no less significant as the standard Soviet tank of the late 1950s and early 1960s, and as with the previous T-54 tank, derivative vehicles and prototypes based on the T-55 tank chassis included bridge launchers, armoured repair and recovery vehicles, and flamethrower tanks, together with a number of development prototypes.

ARMOURED ENGINEER VEHICLES

MTU-20 TANK BRIDGE-LAYER (OBIEKT-602)

The Soviet Army had been provided with an armoured bridge-layer on the T-54 chassis designed to maintain mobility and pace with armoured formations that could keep up with tanks, but the 12-metre-long bridge, mounted on the MTU-12, was too short for many obstacles in the European section of the Soviet Union. As a result, OKB-174 under the direction of Morov began work on creating a bridge-layer with a longer 20-metre-span bridge mounted on the new T-55 tank chassis, with folding end sections that permitted the new bridge still to be transported on standard rail cars.

Under the leadership of designer B. I. Beskupsky, a new bridge was designed with longer folding sections at each end and a new internal layout to provide greater strength. Officially tasked to OKB-174 (KBTM) on 30 May 1960, the new vehicle was designated Obiekt-602 during development and work proceeded on creating two separate variants. The first was a

The original TShM improved bridge-layer prototype, with the longer 20-metre bridge assembly.

TOP The bridge was somewhat unwieldy even with the folded ramps, but it could be manipulated by the layer vehicle.

MIDDLE The bridge would be difficult to move when opened except on open ground.

BOTTOM Even when opened and extended, the chassis provided a sufficient counterweight to balance the bridge when launching it.

50-metric-tonne-class tank assault bridge (Tankovyy Shturmovyy Most or TShM), designated Obiekt-602, while the second was a 60-metric-tonne-class sectional bridge (Razbornyy Most or RMB), the variant fitted with the RMB bridge being designated Obiekt-602A. The latter was a set of four chassis, each carrying a sectional bridge, similar to a tank-mounted version of the lighter truck-mounted KMM and TMM sectional bridges, the set being able to cross obstacles of up to 40 metres in four 10-metre sections but with trestle legs underneath them for additional support. In development the prototypes were designated 'TShM bridge-layer' and 'RMB bridge-layer'.

TOP LEFT The new bridge was particularly sturdy and had no problems with 40-metric-tonne capacity, such as this T-54 crossing the emplaced bridge.

CENTRE LEFT Once the bridge was opened and locked into place, launching it was not a major problem.

BOTTOM LEFT With a few minor modifications, the TShM was accepted into service as the MTU-20.

BELOW This MTU-20, preserved at the Stalin Line Museum in Belarus, shows the sturdy locking mechanism for the bridge ramps.

After testing and development, the Obiekt-602 prototype with the TShM assault bridge was accepted for service with the Soviet Army on 12 November 1964 as the MTU-20. The vehicle weighed 37 metric tonnes and the TShM bridge another 7 metric tonnes. The 20-metre-long cantilever bridge could cross a gap of 18 metres with 1 metre of support on each end or about 16 metres over a less prepared site with 2.2 metres on each end. The bridge was 3.3 metres wide to accommodate nearly all tracked vehicles in service with the Soviet Union at the time of its introduction. Three and a half metres of the bridge folded up to reduce its overall travel length to 11.64 metres.

The bridge, like the previous MTU-12 and the pre-War IT-28 prototype, was launched using a frame and a sturdy winch that pulled the bridge forward on the frame, with hydraulics used for the end ramps and bridge

ABOVE LEFT Hydraulic cylinders and braces were used to hold the twin treadways in alignment with each other.
ABOVE RIGHT The mounts for holding the bridge were likewise robust and durable.
RIGHT Note that the unditching log assembly and brackets have been removed – it appears the Soviet army trusted it would not get stuck!

adjustments. The first step was unfolding the end sections into place before launching. The bridge was then extended to the front of the tank to its limits. The far end was lowered into place and then the vehicle would reverse until it could lower the frame and place the near end on the ground. Recovery was reversed, with the launcher vehicle moving forward to engage the near end of the bridge and lift it off the ground with the frame and then winch the bridge back on to the launcher vehicle.

The chassis retained most of the features of the T-55 chassis such as the SKZ, PPO, TDA and infrared driving capabilities. It had either an R-113 or an R-123 radio set and the R-120 intercom system for its crew of two. Speed was, however, reduced to only 25–30km/h when carrying the bridge.

Due to the size of the TShM bridge design relative to the T-55 chassis, the bridge was constructed of duraluminium alloy to reduce weight. It was found during operational trials, however, that the durability of the bridge was low

TOP LEFT The ramp sections are designed to lie completely flat against the surface of the main section to prevent metal fatigue.

ABOVE Similar to the very first medium bridge-layer built by the Soviet Union in the 1930s, the IT-28, a transmission and differential are used to power heavy chain drives that are used to launch and recover the bridge.

LEFT A later production MTU-1 launcher vehicle with the bridge removed, showing how the guidance cradle for the bridge is mounted on the launcher. The MTU-1 was built primarily on the T-54 chassis, but a small number used the later T-55 chassis.

when large numbers of tanks passed over it. Consequently, though the bridge-layer was accepted for service and 1,222 were built from the beginning of production in 1967, it was largely maintained as reserve inventory for wartime use, and, as with the IS-3 heavy tank, many were exported. The search for an 'everyday' bridge-layer to replace the MTU-12 continued. The very different Obiekt-602A RMB bridging system was built for trials purposes and evaluated by the Soviet Army, but did not progress further.

MTU-55 (MT-55/55A) BRIDGE-LAYER VEHICLE

The MTU-55 was developed at the KB of UVZ as a replacement for the MTU-20 'Mostoukladchik' or bridge-layer. The two-section scissors-type bridge-layer based on the T-55 tank chassis was designed as a collaborative effort between UVZ in Nizhny Tagil and plants in Czechoslovakia, the German DDR and Poland as a standardized bridge-layer for all Warsaw Pact countries. The 16-metre-span bridge was deployed by means of a large stabilizing 'jack' and 'hinge' assembly at the front of the tank with hydraulic operation of the bridge assembly. One of the engineering developments in

TOP LEFT An MT-55 bridge-layer on exercise. While about the same height overall as the MTU-20, the MT-55 was more compact and easier to manoeuvre with the bridge in place.

TOP RIGHT The same MT-55 next to an MT-T based engineering vehicle.

ABOVE The MTU chassis can be forded, as can be seen by the two-section snorkel stowed on the plate over the turret race of the base chassis.

ABOVE LEFT This MT-55, designated a BLG-60 in East German service, is part of the collection of armoured vehicles at Münster. This one shows its launcher without the bridge in place.

LEFT The launcher is hydraulically operated, using powerful hydraulic cylinders to extend and hold the bridge; a semi-automatic system unfolds and locks the bridge as it is erected.

the 1950s that allowed the development of these more advanced bridging systems was the introduction of high-pressure hydraulic systems for engineering-related armoured vehicles, which also saw the development of such vehicles as the IMR.

TOP LEFT Equipment has been rearranged, such as the headlights and fuel tanks on this chassis. The four chocks appear to be an East German addition.

TOP RIGHT This vehicle is on display at the Technical Museum in Togliatti in the Russian Federation. It appears that the bridge unfolding system has been disconnected and can be seen below the lower section of the bridge.

CENTRE LEFT The bridge unfolding piston assembly is more visible in this photo.

CENTRE RIGHT Note that the vehicle commander has both a new direct vision viewer and a cupola to monitor launching and recovery operations from under cover.

BOTTOM LEFT Another MT-55, this one at the Stalin Line Museum in Belarus. It is in better condition than the Togliatti example.

BOTTOM RIGHT With the launching brace retracted, the vehicle retains a decent profile for crossing obstacles, as nothing projects that can dig into an embankment.

The 50-metric-tonne-class bridge weighed 6.5 metric tonnes and could be deployed in three minutes, with an option to join bridge sections together and also build a bridge underwater. The vehicle as built at UVZ in Nizhny Tagil was designated MTU-55. As built in Czechoslovakia, the design was known as the MT-55, and in East Germany as the BLG-60M2. A total of 1,222 MTU-55 (MT-55A) vehicles were built in Omsk.

TOP LEFT The IMR was the first dedicated engineering vehicle capable of being used as a bulldozer, grab, or backhoe as well as emergency recovery vehicle if necessary.

TOP RIGHT The blade assembly was a folding device that could be assembled to form a straight mouldboard, angled plough, or slanted blade at the operator's selection. It folded for travel.

ABOVE The vehicle had a crew of two – namely driver-mechanic and operator/commander. Both were provided with NBC protection to operate in irradiated areas such as the aftermath of a nuclear explosion.

ABOVE RIGHT Here is the same IMR with the backhoe bucket fitted to its multi-purpose extending boom.

MT-55 BRIDGE-LAYER VEHICLE

The MT-55 bridge-layer is effectively the same bridge-layer as the MTU-55 designed by UVZ and described above, but optimized for production at the ZTS factory in Martin, Czechoslovakia. It appears to have been based on the US M48 AVLB with a scissors-folding bridge and operated in the same basic manner.

Design work began in 1962, but it was only in 1967 that five pre-production models were built and underwent testing. Series production began in 1969. A total of 1,762 MT-55 and MT-55A vehicles were built on the T-55 and T-55A chassis respectively, with some being delivered back to the Soviet Army. Another 301 vehicles were delivered to the East German Nationalvolksarmee (NVA) for use as the chassis for their similar BLG-60-series bridge-layer as described above.

The bridge was 16 metres long and was launched by first lowering a wide stabilizing 'jack and hinge' assembly to the ground, as for the Soviet MTU-55. The bridge was configured to open up as it was erected and then was fully extended before it was laid in place. This system could be deployed in three minutes, with recovery also being a matter of only a few minutes.

IMR ENGINEER OBSTACLE CLEARING VEHICLE (OBIEKT-616)

Probably the best-known T-55 derivative vehicle is the Inzhenirnaya Mashina Razgrazhdeniya or Engineer Obstacle Clearing Vehicle, usually abbreviated to IMR, though also known in documents as the ASM emergency rescue vehicle.

Also designed in Omsk by KBTM (Plant No. 174), the IMR was developed as Obiekt-616 (Obiekt-616A) and after testing was approved for service in 1969. The hull and chassis for the IMR were built at Omsk, with the engineering equipment and associated hydraulic systems being fitted at the Novokramatorskiy Machinery Construction Plant. A total of 1,271 of

BELOW LEFT The IMR could be used to both clear roads and make roads in soft ground as needed.

BELOW RIGHT Originally the IMR was used to make firing scrapes for tanks, but after the introduction of the deployable blades for the T-64 and later tanks this function was not required so often.

BOTTOM LEFT The grab claw could be used to either rip down trees or debris or pick them up and remove them from roads or other channels of advance.

BELOW Here an IMR is using the grab to remove debris from a damaged steel reinforced concrete structure.

TOP LEFT The upper hull of the IMR was quite different from the base T-55, and most of the fittings were either eliminated or replaced. The folding travel brace for the arm as well as its reinforcing braces for heavy use are seen stowed on the engine deck.

TOP RIGHT Another view of the same vehicle, showing the straight mouldboard option for the blade.

BOTTOM LEFT The IMR is removing small trees that were knocked down and blocking the way.

BOTTOM RIGHT Here a group of new trainees are receiving instruction on the IMR from an officer.

these unique vehicles were built between 1969 and 1979. The IMR was retroactively designated IMR-1 when a new version on the T-72 chassis, designated IMR-2, appeared in 1991.

The IMR vehicle used the complete hull of the T-55 tank but with a rotating armoured mounting replacing the turret. It had a crew of two; driver-mechanic and commander-operator. Since one of its primary reasons for creation was clearing of obstacles and debris resulting from potential nuclear detonations, the vehicle was from the outset provided with an anti-radiation liner (*podboy*) and SKZ overpressure system.

The IMR was fitted with several particularly useful hydraulically operated devices for its intended purpose. At the front was a large flexible bulldozer blade, which could be angled to use as a 3.4-metre-wide road grader or straightened out to serve as a 4.15-metre-wide bulldozer, as employed on earlier but far less specialized engineering vehicles such as the BAT-1. When split 'snowplough' style the blade could sweep a width of 3.56 metres. It was also capable of clearing heavy snow at 200–300 metres/hour or landslides at 160–200 metres/hour.

The IMR's 'star performer' was a multi-purpose extendable boom with a maximum reach of up to 8.8 metres, which was provided with a choice of two fittings: either a special claw assembly that could be used to lift trees or debris,

(1) The grab device could lift large obstacles a good distance off the ground.

(2) The reach of the arm with the grab in place was more than eight metres.

(3) For longer distances, the IMR was loaded on a flatbed transporter.

(4) This vehicle is part of the collection of the Artillery and Engineering Museum in St. Petersburg. This particular one is in good condition.

(5) The St. Petersburg IMR is preserved with the grab, probably the most common fitting, in place on the arm.

(6) The IMR operates on hydraulics, and the hoses for the hydraulic control systems are seen here.

(7) The blade assembly is structurally robust and has significant bracing behind it to prevent buckling or damage to the hull.

(8) Note that the backhoe bucket is stowed in sections on the rear of the hull.

(9) The arm has a range of motion of almost 360°, but cannot be fully swung fully around due to the hydraulic connections and fittings.

(10) The operator's cab has a number of heavy armoured glass viewers to permit operation under NBC conditions, but as noted they were found to be ineffective at Chernobyl and had to be sealed, vehicle control then being by means of remote control cameras.

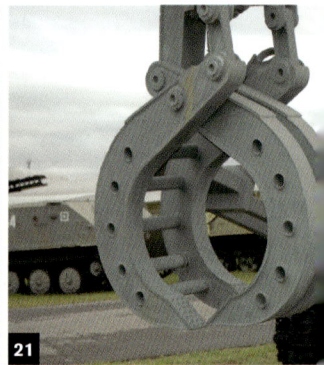

(11) The rear of the arm, showing its cradle and mounting trunnions.

(12) Another preserved IMR, this time mounted on a plinth as a memorial.

(13) This vehicle has a slightly different backhoe bucket as well as a guard around the operator's cab and fitting next to the arm.

(14) Another IMR, this time in the collection at Technical Museum collection at Togliatti. Some of the track-guard stowage and fittings have been removed.

(15) The heavy duty nature of the bulldozer control pistons and brackets is obvious here.

(16) The fronts of the track guards were fitted with deflector devices to protect stowed items from damage due to soil or debris striking them during movement.

(17) The fittings for a 95-litre external fuel tank and hoses are visible on the right fender.

(18) More of the fittings and brackets on the right side of the vehicle are visible, even though their items are missing.

(19) The IMR is a 'one-stop shop' for most non-construction tactical engineering work and is fitted out to that end, but as noted most of its external equipment is missing here.

(20) Rear fittings, such as the unditching log, are also no longer present.

(21) The massive construction and 'scissors' operation of the grab can be seen in this photo.

or a backhoe bucket of 0.4m³ capacity that was capable of moving up to 40m³ of soil per hour. The boom-in-claw mode could lift large pieces of debris or fallen trees up to 2 metric tonnes in weight.

While the vehicles performed yeoman work in exercises and were deployed on behalf of Soviet forces such as Afghanistan, they were also called to the fore in 1986 when Chernobyl Reactor No. 4 exploded and melted down. Dozens of IMR vehicles were rushed to the site to assist in clearing rubble and helping create the 'sarcophagus' to seal the crippled reactor.

As was reported by Soviet armoured vehicle troubleshooter Yuri Kostenko, the radiation cladding on IMR and other Soviet armoured vehicles involved in the emergency response proved insufficient when exposed to the massive neutron radiation coming from the melted pile. Crews were irradiated very quickly and many died from that radiation poisoning. As an emergency measure, Soviet Army engineers lined the vehicles with lead, removed all external vision devices and replaced them with remote control cameras, and then strictly limited the time of exposure to less than 30 minutes per session. The emergency was, however, unprecedented, and the engineering solutions available in such circumstances were limited.

Due to the levels of radiation encountered, the IMR vehicles, as with all military vehicles used in the cleanup at Chernobyl, were impossible to decontaminate. While the IMR vehicles did great work clearing the debris and helping to seal the reactor, all of the vehicles used were thereby subsequently abandoned among the 6,000 vehicles and a number of helicopters, many of which have remained parked in a nearby abandoned airfield to the present day.

BMR-2 MINE CLEARING VEHICLE

The Boevaya Mashina Razminirovaniya-2 (BMR-2) or mine clearing vehicle Model 2 was originally designed based on the T-54B tank chassis, but it is understood that conversions were carried out on both the T-54B and later T-55 chassis as these were undertaken in the Soviet Union in the 1980s.

The BMR-2 was developed at the No. 482 Design Technology Centre in Kiev, for implementation on converted later T-54B and T-55 chassis, with conversion work undertaken at No. 17 Bronetankovoy Zavod (BTZ) in Lvov. The vehicle superficially resembled the earlier BMR-1, which was built on the chassis of SU-122-54 tank destroyers with their 122mm guns removed and with a road-wheel layout in turn reconfigured from the base T-54 tank.

The BMR-2 mounted the KMT-7 'Panas' mine trawl, which took 3.5 hours to install and 20 minutes to dismount. The vehicle was converted in considerable numbers, and saw belated service in the War In Ukraine that started in 2014.

(1) The BMR-2 with its arms in place but no mine rollers rigged to them.

(2) For travel, the mine rollers stow in racks on the engine deck when in administrative travel mode.

(3) The BMR-2 only carries two sets of mine rollers, with replacement sets being carried on trucks following in the rear. It also has a lane marker to show cleared pathways to other vehicles (box behind the auxiliary fuel tanks). Also note the MTP-3 recovery vehicle in the background.

(4) The vehicle carries all of the late model T-55 upgrades, including a set of 12 Type 902A 'Tucha' smoke grenade launchers, an NVST or 'Kord' 12.7mm heavy machine gun,

hoses directly connecting the auxiliary fuel tanks to the chassis fuel system, and the steel reinforced side skirts.

(5) To install the rollers, the vehicle moves to a secure area behind the line of contact.

(6) A crane and jib (carried on the vehicle) are erected to lift the roller assemblies out of their travel racks (these appear to be civilian workers).

(7) This vehicle is also having its arms changed or installed first.

(8) Once rigged, the rollers are swung out over the side and moved to the front.

(9) When in place, the BMR-2's chains and cables are hooked up, fastening the rollers to the arms.

(10) The vehicle then moves out to carry out its mine clearing mission.

(11) Mine sweeping was carried out at relatively low speeds, both to ensure thorough coverage and to prevent major damage to the vehicle when it did strike a mine.

(12) When it did strike a mine, the results would depend on its size and type. This BRM-2 appears to either have struck a heavy anti-tank mine or an IED, which has flipped the rollers over completely, twisting the arm and damaging the vehicle.

(13) Another view of the same vehicle, showing the damage.

(14) In some cases, the vehicle itself would be damaged by the blast; this one has suffered major damage to the second road wheel station on the right side.

(15) While barely visible in this head-on shot, the BMR-2 was fitted with the hull floor standoff armour from the BDD package to protect the driver-mechanic and crew from mine explosions.

(16) A 'posterity' photo of a fully equipped BMR-2 minus its arms.

(17) The crew of the BMR-2 was only two men, but in Afghanistan they were usually also augmented by a trained mine dog and handlers to seek out IEDs, which the mujahedin might not want to detonate under the mine sweeper, waiting instead for a tank or fuel tanker.

T-55 tanks awaiting conversion to secondary vehicle types such as the BMR-2 mine clearance vehicle.

BELOW The prototype TMT jet engine mine clearer, with the massive assembly on the rear deck and ducting of the jet efflux forward.

BELOW RIGHT The TMT from the front, showing the jet exhaust ducts angled downward to clear a track-width path of mines. Rollers and ploughs were found to work better and also not to give the vehicle away by a high noise level, as did the jet engine.

TMT JET-PROPELLED MINE CLEARING VEHICLE (OBIEKT-604)

One of the more obscure derivative vehicles based on the T-55 chassis was the Turboreaktivnyy Minnyy Tral'shchik (TMT) or Jet-Propelled Mine Clearer. Developed under a Resolution from the SM SSSR dated 25 October 1961, the project was executed by Morov and OKB-174 in Omsk as Obiekt-604, on which the lead designer was A. A. Lyakhov.

This vehicle used the hull and driveline of the T-55 tank with only one major change, namely moving the three centre road wheels forward and leaving the fifth mount in place so that the hull looked to be reversed. The vehicle had a completely new superstructure design. The lower hull was now divided into a control compartment, two jet engine compartments, fuel tanks, and the engine-transmission compartment. The TMT carried 1,500 litres of TS-1 kerosene (jet fuel) for its two R11F-300 jet engines. Armour protection was reduced to 80mm on the glacis and 45mm on the sides.

The vehicle had two large nozzles to vector the jet exhaust down and forward to sweep the area in front of each track. The jet exhaust streams were

calculated to clear an area four metres wide and up to 300–500mm deep in soil and 600mm in snow. Due to the nature of the engines, a second PPO fire suppression system was added to prevent fires involving the jet engines. The vehicle was also fitted with a PAZ overpressure nuclear protection system.

The TMT vehicle had reduced fuel capacity and thus only had a range of 130–190 kilometres. There is no information on how long the jet engines could run; sweeping speed was only 3–4 km/h. Due to the huge clouds of dust kicked up while operating, the driver-mechanic was provided with a GPK-48 gyrocompass to keep him on course. Although tested for service in late 1963, the Obiekt-604 (TMT) was not accepted for service. A similar system was tested on the K-90 amphibious light tank, the predecessor to the PT-76.

OTHER ENGINEER-RELATED VEHICLES

There are some speciality engineer vehicles, such as the BAT and BAT-M combat engineer vehicles or the MDK-2 trench-digging vehicle. These are wholly new chassis but used T-44/T-54 parts when built (mostly a down-rated V-2 engine variant and the driveline and tracked drive components) and were upgraded to T-55 components of the same type when rebuilt. There are also numerous post-Soviet variants such as high intensity tracked GPM-type firefighting vehicles using both T-54 and T-55 chassis and speciality engineering and crane vehicles, but with the exception of the GPM vehicles none are directly related to the original T-55 and its derivative vehicles.

A conversion of a T 55 to a GPM firefighting vehicle chassis. These chassis exist using various base vehicles and are proposed for use as surface to air missile systems, associated radars, or civilian/military dual use such as cranes or fire fighting equipment.

ATTACHED ENGINEER EQUIPMENT

MINE AND OBSTACLE CLEARING DEVICES

PT-55 Mine Trawl

This mine trawl, while designed for use on the T-55 tank, was a further development of the PT-54 device and compatible with earlier T-54 tanks. Developed in 1959, it weighed 6.7 to 7 metric tonnes, but only cleared a strip 0.83 metres wide in front of each track and could only withstand 10 equivalent TM-46 blasts. It did not penetrate the ground as deeply as previous models.

Manoeuvrability was poor: turning the tank in a mine field required a turn radius of 85 metres, and even outside the mine field with neutral steer-style turning it took a radius of 9 metres to turn around.

The PT-55 took 10 to 15 minutes to install with a crane, and dismounting took 3 to 5 minutes. However, the speed of travel was quicker with the PT-55 and clearing speeds of 15–20 km/h were noted. The PT-55 system required three trucks to carry, including the marker assembly that was fitted at the rear of the hull to show the path cleared by the tank.

Most of the later-designed mine trawls such as the KMT-4 and KMT-5 could also be mounted on T-54 and T-55 tanks fitted to use mine trawl equipment.

KMT-4 Mine Trawl

The universal attachment fittings on the T-55 tanks could also be used for one of a number of mine clearing devices, universally called 'trawls' by the Russians. The term KMT expands as 'Koleynyy Minoviranyy Traul' or 'track-width mine trawl'. This particular device is actually a mine plough. These are rake-shaped devices placed in front of each track run and set to run deep enough to force a buried mine to the surface and deflect it away from the tank.

The KMT-4 was developed by OKB-200 at Plant No. 78 in Chelyabinsk per a Resolution from the SM SSSR. It was designed for use on either T-54 or T-55 tanks and was accepted for service with the Soviet Army in 1962. It used hydraulic cylinders to lift the plough sections or lower them for use. Each one was 1.1 metres wide and could dig up mines buried up to 600mm below the surface. It added 1.1 metric tonnes to the weight of the tank.

An improved model, the KMT-4M, was introduced in 1966 and used pneumatic control for the elevating pistons.

KMT-5 Mine Trawl

Whereas the KMT-4 was a plough, the KMT-5 was a more traditional roller detonation mine trawl. Also created at the same time as the KMT-4 by

OKB-200 at Plant No. 78 in Chelyabinsk, the KMT-5 was adopted in 1962 at the same time as its sibling apparatus.

This device consists of two sets of three heavy cast steel wheels carried on frames that projected ahead of the tank and were trailed by two two-bladed mine ploughs. A heavy metal roller on a chain linked the two sections together and was set there to detonate trip-rod-type mines before they were detonated by the tank's hull. The trawl projected some 3.18 metres in front of the tank, but, due to its construction, once installed it could not be lifted out of the way by the tank's driver-mechanic.

Each section cleared a strip of 710–810mm wide at a sweeping speed of 6–12 km/h. The complete trawl weighed 7.5 metric tonnes. It took a crane and 3.5 hours to install, but could be removed in 20 minutes; in an emergency it could be detached by the tank crew in less than one minute. The tank's manoeuvrability was severely limited when using the mine trawl.

The trawl was designed to roll over and detonate mines by pressure, and the estimated life expectancy of each roller section was six detonations by Soviet TM-57-class anti-tank mines. A detonation would throw the mine trawl into the air and required the tank to back up 2–3 metres to reset the trawl in operating position.

ENGINEER EQUIPMENT

BTU STANDARDIZED TANK BULLDOZER

Like the US and Great Britain, both of which had fitted bulldozer blades to standard tanks for use in combat situations for obstacle clearing, road smoothing, filling in craters and bunkers under fire, and digging positions for use by tanks and SP guns for defensive fires, the Soviet Army also decided it needed a bulldozer fitting for its medium tanks.

A blade system was developed specifically for the T-54, and designed for fitment to the bow of line tanks without any major redesign required of the tank. This bulldozer had a mouldboard with a width of 3.4 metres and a depth of 1.1 metres with a built-in folding depth control shoe in the centre of the blade. The tank could plough to a depth of 0.2 metres per pass with the shoe in place or 0.45 metres with it folded. The tank in this situation could move 100 to 230m³ of earth per hour. This would permit one tank to dig 3 to 5 defensive positions per hour for tanks.

Fitting the bulldozer assembly to the tank took 1.5–2 hours, but removing it only required only 30–40 minutes. Dropping the blade from travel to working position took five seconds. The driver-mechanic had the blade

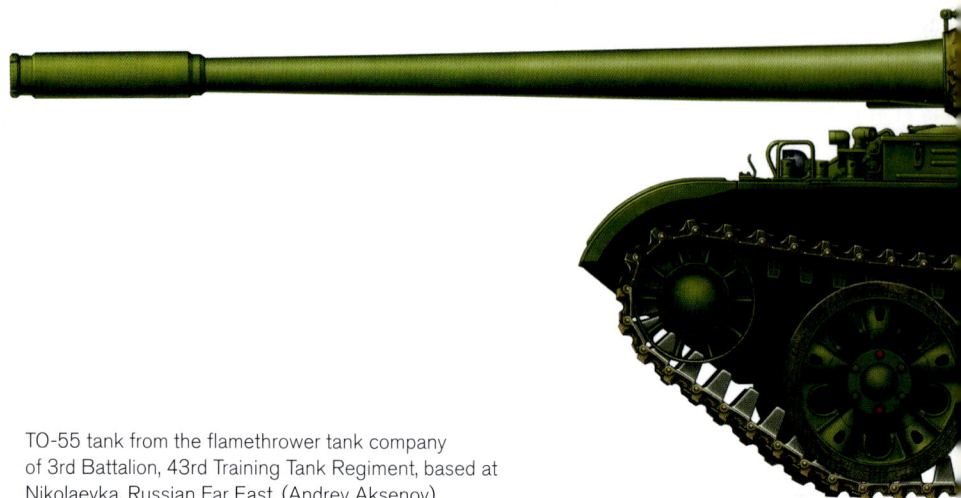

TO-55 tank from the flamethrower tank company of 3rd Battalion, 43rd Training Tank Regiment, based at Nikolaevka, Russian Far East. (Andrey Aksenov)

controls attached to his control levers inside the tank. The blade was raised and lowered by chains attached to hydraulic cylinders. The blade weighed 2.3 metric tonnes, and when installed limited top speed to 16–18 km/h in travel mode or 3–6 km/h in working mode

The BTU-54 was replaced by the similar BTU-55 in 1963, but either one could be fitted to a T-54 tank with the required mounting points. These were the 12 fittings attached to the upper (four) and lower (eight) glacis of the tank. No major specialized fittings or equipment other than the standardized mounts needed to be carried by any T-54 or T-55 tank.

These blades were not suitable for use as snowploughs, however, even though they were often used for that work. Part of the reason was that it was difficult to move the snow to one side or the other and thus it just piled up in front of the tank. The British Military Liaison Mission (BRIXMIS) forwarded one unclassified photo of an East German NVA T-55 with BTU-55 that was completely buried up to the machine gun mount in snow while trying to be used for road clearing in the 1978–79 New Year's Blizzard in East Germany.

In later years, Soviet main battle tanks such as the T-72 and T-80 were fitted with a compact 'samookapivaniya' or self-digging bulldozer blade on the lower glacis, which was hydraulically lowered as required to allow the tank to dig its own emplacement. The prototype system for this future development was built and evaluated on the T-55 chassis. However, while good for emplacement of tanks it was not suitable for use as a general purpose bulldozer and those functions had to be carried out by other vehicles.

FLAMETHROWER TANKS

TO-55 FLAMETHROWER TANK (OBIEKT-482)

As with the TO-54 flamethrower tank based on the T-54 chassis, a need for a flame weapon mounted on the new T-55 chassis was also recognized. Development of this tank was tasked to Plant No. 75 in Kharkov and chief designer Morozov, who assigned direct supervision of the task to M. S. Ozersky in collaboration with the Omsk KB.

Initially the design was based on the T-54B tank and designated Obiekt-482. Prototypes were produced in late 1958 and tested between March and July 1959. On 17 January 1960, the vehicle was accepted for service with the Soviet Army, but now on the new T-55 tank chassis as the TO-55 (Tyazhelaya Ognemetnaya-55) or heavy flamethrower (T)-55. Starting in 1961, and as with most derivative T-55 variants, production was transferred to Plant No. 174 in Omsk. Between 1957 and 1963 some 830 of these tanks were produced.

The main difference in armament between this tank, which retained the standard 100mm D-10T2S main armament, and the TO-54 was that it mounted the improved ATO-200 flamethrower, still as a co-axial weapon in place of the 7.62mm SGMT machine gun, and carried 460 litres of flame mixture under armour. This was a superior weapon to the earlier ATO-1 and could project

A later production (or possibly upgraded) TO-55 tank with the AAMG and the flame gun in place.

A TO-55 fires a burst from the flamethrower. The main problem was range, as even with a powerful compressor and new flame gun the range was only 160–200 metres at maximum. The solution was found to be encapsulated flame mixtures like those used in the RPO-A 'Shmel" launcher.

flame bursts to 160–200 metres horizontally (based on weather conditions such as wind direction and speed) and up to the 5th floor of a building at ranges of 130–160 metres. However, wind conditions of 3 metres/second or more (about 7 mph) knocked the horizontal range down to only 110 metres.

The tank could use any one of four flame mixtures, SKS-O, SKS-15, SKS-30 or BBTs. The latter used OP-2 powder as an additive. The tank could fire 25 bursts of flame.

The basic load for the main gun was reduced from 43 rounds to 25 and only 750 rounds for the bow 7.62mm SGMT machine gun. There were 12 propellant and 12 igniter cartridges for the flamethrower. These provided a total of 12 bursts of around 38 litres per burst.

Beginning in 1969, the TO-55 was also fitted out with the 12.7mm DShKM machine gun mount on the turret roof, with 300 rounds for that weapon, and KTD-1 / KTD-2 laser rangefinders were also latterly added to some tanks.

The fuel capacity was reduced from 680 to 465 litres and the range to only 380–400 kilometres without the auxiliary fuel tanks.

The TO-55 was removed from Russian Army inventory in 1993.

ARMAMENT VARIATIONS AND UPGRADES

T-55 WITH 9K11 'MALYUTKA' ANTI-TANK GUIDED MISSILE SYSTEM (OBIEKT-614V)

The T-55 was, as described earlier, experimentally fitted between 1961 and 1963 with a turret rear-mounted 'cage' with three 9M14 'Malyutka' missiles for the 9K11 ATGM system. The original Obiekt-614A system was developed on the basis of the T-54A tank by OKB-174 at Plant No. 174 from 1961 under the direction of Morov, with the Obiekt-614B development being tested on the T-54B. The system was later modified at Plant No. 183 on the basis of the T-55A tank, as the Obiekt-614V, with the launcher system being altered and the number of rockets carried within the tank increased. The launcher and its protective frame 'cage' were now mounted higher on the turret rear rather than being folded behind the turret and raised for launch, which reduced preparation time for engagement to under 30 seconds. The 9M14 rockets were directed towards their target via a 9V332 control point mounted within the turret and aimed via a TShB-22 tank sight. The modified system was installed on the T-55 tank from October to December 1964 at the NIIBT Polygon at Kubinka. Development continued on the T-62 and other tank chassis, but was ultimately

1

2

3

4

5

(1) The early model TO-55 on display at the Kubinka Tank Museum. This was a straight replacement of the co-axial machine gun with the flame weapon.

(2) There were no major characteristics other than the flame gun shroud to differentiate the tank from line T-55 tanks.

(3) The nozzle is protected by a heavy cast shroud to prevent damage from shell fragments.

(4) The flame nozzle is connected to the main gun and searchlight linkage by a heavy arm to keep all three in synchronization when the gun is elevated.

(5) The range of the flame stream was limited by wind, pressure and elevation of the main gun.

The T-55, as experimentally fitted with a three-rail launcher for the 9M14 'Malyutka' anti-tank guided missile. While the concept worked, it had too many drawbacks to make it viable.

One of the problems was sighting the missile, as it had to fire over the top of the turret, and the gunner had to acquire a missile that was heading upwards and not forwards. He used his sight and viewer to guide the missile to the target.

not standardized on any Soviet tank. Thirty systems were built on the T-62 MBT for long-term service evaluation purposes.

While Plant No. 183 worked on the 9K11 'Malyutka' ATGM systems mounted on the T-55A tank for development purposes, the KB at Plant No. 183 under Kartsev in June 1962 also developed the engineering drawings for a T-55 variant mounting the 9M12 'Ovod' guided ATGM developed by TsKB-14 in Tula. The 9M12 'Ovod' rocket was a 'lightweight' alternative to the 9M17 'Skorpion', which had been in development for some time. The 'Ovod' ATGM used the same mounting arrangements as for the smaller 9M14 'Malyutka' ATGM, but located in a lightly armoured container. This system did not progress beyond a feasibility study and was abandoned due to the parallel development of an alternative through-barrel launched ATGM, which would later enter service as the 9K116 'Bastion'.

The T-55 chassis was also used during the original development of the 2K4 'Drakon' ATGM system firing the 3M7 rocket. The 2K4 system was originally developed on the Obiekt-140 prototype chassis for ultimate service deployment on the Obiekt-155 (T-55). Kartsev and his team at UVZ in Nizhny Tagil worked with OKB-16 (led by A. E. Nudelman) on the tank chassis for the 2K4 'Drakon', but as protracted development work continued, a production replacement for the T-55 was already in development at UVZ, namely the T-62 MBT. The design chassis for the 2K4 'Drakon' system was thereby changed to the Obiekt-150 based on the new T-62 MBT then in development at UVZ, which was ultimately used as the chassis for the production 2K4 'Drakon' ATGM vehicle that was built in small numbers. The 2K4 'Drakon' was contemplated for installation on the T-55, T-62 and T-64 tank chassis, and also on the Obiekt-167 and Obiekt-167T, but only the T-62-based variant was actually built.

The other major problem was that the missiles were vulnerable to shell fragments or small arms in their exposed position. However, providing an element of armoured protection to the launcher would not solve other problems in addition to this major issue, since the loader was required to exit the tank to reload the missiles in combat, and the missiles deprived the tank of several rounds of more useful 100mm ammunition. The solution was a through-the-bore missile system.

T-55 WITH 100MM 'RAPIRA' SMOOTHBORE TANK GUN

In 1960, the KB at Plant No. 183 developed a project that considered the re-arming of the T-55 with a tank gun variant of the potent 100mm T-12 (2A19) 'Rapira' smoothbore towed anti-tank gun then being readied for service with the Soviet Army. The ballistic properties of the T-12 'Rapira' and its APFSDS anti-tank rounds were impressive, but the unitary rounds proved impossible to manoeuvre within the confines of a T-55 (or any other) Soviet tank turret. The project was therefore abandoned.

ADDITIONAL DEFENSIVE PROTECTION

As secondary armour was being considered at the beginning of the 1960s, the T-55 was experimentally fitted with different forms of additional defensive armour, some of which was later adopted as standard, and some of which was shelved after prototype testing.

T-55 WITH ANTI-CUMULATIVE ROUND APPLIQUÉ SCREEN ARMOUR

In 1960 and 1961, VNII-100 investigated several types of secondary appliqué armour, referred to generically as 'Protivokumulyativnaya Ehkrannaya Zaschita' or anti-cumulative round appliqué protection (also referred to as 'Setchataya Ehkrannaya Zaschita' [SEhZ], or screen [net] armour shielding), which was tested on the T-54, the T-55 and latterly the T-62.

Two types of particularly novel screen 'Ehkrannaya Zaschita' or appliqué armour were developed for the T-54 and T-55 tanks, designated respectively 'Zontik' (umbrella) and 'Shater' (tent). The 'Zontik' system, as the name suggested, consisted of a large-scale folding net umbrella stowed on (around) the gun barrel, which unfolded to form a 360° forward facing 'umbrella', screening the tank over its frontal aspects. The 'Shater' system was a similar but vertically mounted 'tent' or 'yurt' that provided 360° protection for the whole tank including its upper surfaces, long before the advent of indirect flight path guided munitions and attack helicopters. The 'Shater' kit weighed 200kg. Work on these designs later continued with the T-62 and even the T-10M heavy tank.

In parallel with the 'Zontik' and 'Shater' developments, VNII-100 also developed appliqué screens for protecting the side armour and running gear from cumulative rounds. Several alternative side screens or skirts were developed, using screen mesh and combination metal frame and 5mm rubber armour, which added 326kg to the combat weight of the tank. These screens developed at VNII 100 were built at Plant No. 183 and tested at the NIIBT polygon at Kubinka in November and December 1962, using Soviet 85mm and 115mm cumulative rounds for the purpose. Work continued on these various designs on an ongoing basis, with the ЗЭT-1 (ZEhT-1) or 'Zaschita Ehkrannaya Tankovaya' (tank appliqué armour) being tested at the NIIBT polygon at Kubinka in 1964 for use with the T-54, the T-55 and the new T-62. The 'Zontik' and 'Shater' systems were ultimately dropped, but the side skirts featuring combination steel and rubber armour would later become standard on series production T-55M, T-55AM and AMV tanks.

In addition to passive defensive systems, VNII-100 and NII-61 worked in collaboration to develop an active defence system involving ATGMs.

T-55 WITH 'OPLOT-MO' ACTIVE DEFENCE SYSTEM

In parallel with appliqué armour developments, VNII-100 also developed a first generation active defence system in the early 1960s, based on Resolution of the Council of Ministers (SM SSSR) dated 18 February 1960. The system, designated 'Oplot-MO', was developed as a collaborative effort between NII-61, VNII-100 and the Kazansky Aviation Institute. The installation consisted of a six-barrel 12.7mm calibre 'Gatling'-type anti-aircraft machine gun directly linked to an acquisition radar, and mounted for trials purposes on the turret roof of a T-55 medium/main battle tank and a T-10M heavy tank. The 'Oplot-MO' system would engage incoming munitions travelling at 600–800 metres per second at a distance of 200 metres from the tank with an envisaged burst of fire with a combined rate of 10,000 rounds per minute. The system was in continual development during the 1960s and was the precursor to the later 'Drozd' and subsequent Soviet active defence systems.

T-55 TANKS WITH EXPERIMENTAL NIGHT VISION EQUIPMENT

In 1961, two T-55 tanks were fitted with the TPNB-1-22 combination sight for night operation. Trials showed, however, that range with reliable definition was limited to 300 metres at night rather than the 800 metres required according to the original TTT specifications. After rework, two more TPNB-1-22 sights were fitted back in the T-55 test-bed tanks and retested in May and June 1962. Range was at 600 metres a significant improvement, and definition also improved, but was still below original specification. The sight was also vulnerable to damage as the main armament was fired. Development work continued, with the results being incorporated into future night vision sighting systems.

T-55 PROTOTYPES WITH ENGINE UPGRADES

In 1961 and 1962, a modification of the V-55 engine, the V-55M, was developed and tested in the T-55 in the region of Tedzhent in the Turkmenistan Military District (TurkVO) in 1962. The new engine, effectively a 'multi-fuel' engine, was designed to run on Soviet TS-1 and TS-2 kerosene-type aviation fuel, A-66 and A-72 petrol, and other fuels. The T-55 was also tested in the same region in 1965 and 1966, fitted with a V-36 engine.

T-55 PROTOTYPES WITH AUTOMATIC TRANSMISSION (OBIEKT-601, OBIEKT-606)

A project was developed at the KB of Plant No. 174 in Omsk that investigated the potential fitment of an automatic transmission to the T-55. The initial project undertaken from 1959 to 1961 was designated Obiekt-601. The transmission performed well overall, but the main design element that required further modification was identified as gear synchronization. Development continued as the Obiekt-606, of which three prototypes were built. VNII-100 developed the GMT-150 hydromechanical transmission with a potential T-55 application, with work ultimately moving forward with the Obiekt-612, which was based on the later T-62 tank chassis. The original Omsk projects were duly shelved.

T-55 WITH UPGRADED ELECTRICAL SYSTEM (OBIEKT-605)

In 1963, a project was also developed at Omsk considering a new electrical power system for a future tank. The project, designated Obiekt-605, was tested at the NIIBT polygon at Kubinka in 1964.

T-55 PROTOTYPE WITH AUTOLOADER

In 1965, a prototype based on a T-55 'khodovoi maket' (running model) was developed at VNII-100 investigating advanced features that were at the time also being considered for future Soviet main battle tanks. The prototype included an autoloader, a crew reduced to two, which was extreme even by upcoming T-64 and T-72 standards, and, perhaps most unusually, the driver-mechanic located in the turret in a suspended basket, making him less vulnerable to mine blasts on the hull floor. The prototype was also fitted with television video cameras for observation purposes.

BTR-T HEAVY ARMOURED PERSONNEL CARRIER

In the late 1990s the Russians began to look at world armour developments and some of their own more obsolescent tanks, and noted that in Israel the IDF had created the 'Achzarit' heavy APC from their long-since captured T-54 and T-55 tank chassis. As the Russian Federation was now faced with a large number of T-54 and T-55 tanks that as of 1997 were to be scrapped, OKBTM in Omsk began to look at possible conversions for both domestic consumption and potential export at a time of few defence contracts being awarded in the country. One of these was the heavy APC concept that the Israelis had earlier demonstrated.

A new upper hull was designed for the T-55 chassis and from the start featured integrated explosive reactive armour protection. It had a crew of

(1) The Russians were attracted to the concept of a heavy armoured personnel carrier both by observing the IDF in action and by their own unhappy experiences in Chechnya with urban combat. Starting in 1999, KBTM in Omsk offered the BTR-T, a heavy personnel carrier based on the T-55.

(2) While this version did not carry a large 'desant' dismount section – five to seven being the numbers most quoted – it did place them in a protected cell, with double walls of armour with fuel tanks and equipment stowage between them and danger. Large front-opening hatches protected the dismount team on exiting. Later versions added dismount steps at the rear.

(3) A modified tank glacis plate was used with reactive armour modules attached to protect the crew (most likely here with 'Kontakt-5' being used).

(4) A full set of 12 Type 902A 'Tucha' smoke grenade launchers were fitted to the rear sections of the armoured sponson bins.

(5) While the chassis retained the mounts for the 200-litre auxiliary fuel tanks, they were not used with this variant due to the need for crew members to dismount at the rear of the vehicle.

(6) The BTR-T is fitted with a low profile unmanned turret fitted with a 12.7mm NVST or 'Kord' heavy machine gun with remote control. The commander has an access hatch to the right of the gun.

(7) The turret is sloped to the front to provide increased protection.

(8) The BTR-T has the identical mobility of the tank chassis.

(9) The vehicle has a stay-aboard crew of two in addition to the 'desant' team.

(10) While the concept proved sound, eventually the design work moved on to a version based on the T-72 chassis and carrying a full squad-sized (9–11 men) 'desant' team. The design layout of the latter vehicle was virtually identical to the T-55-based prototypes. (All BTR-T photographs Andrey Aksenov)

two, namely driver-mechanic and commander, and could carry a 'desant' crew of 11–13 personnel. A prototype was developed and shown but no interest apparently materialized.

A second design – more like a miniature version of the later 'Ramka' or Obiekt-199, better known as the 'Terminator' – was duly developed. It possessed a modular hull of much lower profile and a sharper bow profile for the glacis and could carry the same two-man crew and a smaller 'desant' crew of five. It was provided with a modular turret capable of mounting a 30mm 2A42 automatic cannon, a twin 30mm 2A38 automatic cannon, a 12.7mm NVST machine gun, an AGS-17-type 30mm automatic grenade launcher, and 9M113 'Konkurs' ATGMs. A prototype of this design was also built but with no further development undertaken.

A command and control '1V' vehicle variant of the original large-casemate vehicle was also proposed and described, but although there have been some limited attempts with the T-80 tank nothing to date has proceeded using the T-55 chassis. New prototypes are on a T-72 chassis and a patent for that particular variant has been filed with the Russian Patent Office.

One of the early 'tank escort vehicles', was originally envisaged on a T-55 based chassis. This later (T-72 based) Obiekt-781 prototype now features twin 30mm 2A72 guns, a 30mm AG-17 grenade launcher on each side of the bow, and what appears to be a two-round ATGM launcher on the right side. This was one option for the vehicle that eventually emerged as the Obiekt-199 'Terminator' combat vehicle on a T-72 or T-90 chassis.

BMO-T HEAVY FLAMETHROWER VEHICLE

As with the BTR-T, another vehicle that KBTM proposed and offered was the BMO heavy flamethrower vehicle. But in contrast with previous flamethrower vehicles, which mounted a projector and a set amount of flammable fuel, the new vehicle was designed to carry up to 33 RPO-A handheld projectile type projectors for use by a five-man 'desant' or dismount team.

The vehicle was similar in design to the BTR-T but featured a shorter casemate and sharper front profile. It was provided with a cupola armed with a 12.7mm NSVT heavy machine gun for the commander. The RPO-A tubes (using a clip-on launcher handle and mechanism with the tubes being discarded after use) were stowed within the casemate as well as in armoured compartments on either side of the hull.

The RPO-A 'Shmel" (bumblebee) is actually a thermobaric type weapon rather than a traditional flamethrower. It creates a cloud of vaporized fuel when it bursts that is then ignited by a detonator, causing a massive fireball; once all of the fuel is consumed along with the oxygen in the area, a vacuum is created that sucks in any items that can be moved or crushed by the pressure, so it is a 'two for one' weapon capable of levelling a frame house, killing everyone in a room or bunker (or cave) and also penetrating and killing all personnel in an armoured vehicle without hermetic sealing.

The original BMO-T as developed for the T-55 chassis was not developed further, but work continued on the basis of the T-72 tank chassis, in which form it entered service with the Chemical Troops of the Russian Federation. The T-72-based BMO-T is in production and is issued in platoons of three vehicles each to units with allocated chemical companies. Each new Russian brigade has one such company and divisions retain chemical battalions.

REPAIR AND RECOVERY VEHICLES

While the Soviet Union used the T-54 and T-55 for many different derivative vehicles, they were never used as a dedicated repair and recovery vehicle. The T-54 did have some BTS-2 variants for recovery and minor repairs, and later T-44s were completely rebuilt to serve as the more developed BTS-4.

This was not the case with the other three major T-54/T-55 producers – Poland, the CSSR, and China. All three did create dedicated repair and recovery vehicles. The main difference between them and the Soviet BTS vehicles was a large and powerful crane to pull engines, transmissions, turrets, main guns, and any other heavy items without the need of a repair train. All the BTS vehicles could do was drag a disabled machine back to a collection point or carry out minor to mid-level repairs in the field, depending on how many mechanics and spare parts it carried.

The Poles had several, of which the best known was the WZT-2; at least 600 were built. The Czechs built 2,321 similar VT-55 vehicles for domestic and export use (some of which reportedly re-exported to the Soviet Union). The Chinese version, based on the Type 59, was the Type 653.

All of them were marked by having a heavy brace or spade (WZT and Type 653 front, VT-55 rear) and a large and powerful winch in the centre of

BELOW A late model Ukrainian-built BTS-5 recovery and repair vehicle based on a T-55 chassis.

BELOW LEFT A Czech VT-55 vehicle as used by the East German NVA and now in the collection at Münster.

the hull, plus a crane offset to one side for use in heavy maintenance or repair. Extra bins and containers carried tools, spare parts or replacement parts as needed. Many secondary users like Iraq would combine them with T-54/T-55 units and it was not out of the ordinary to find Soviet, Polish, Czech and Chinese vehicles in a single regiment.

It was much later that the Soviets created the BREhM-1 vehicle on the T-72 chassis for the same purposes with a crane and winch plus spades and cargo racks.

'PLAVSREDSTVA' AMPHIBIOUS WATER CROSSING MEANS

In 1962, experiments were conducted on providing the T-55 tank with the means for crossing significant water obstacles such as large lakes or even areas of open sea close to shore. The original experiments conducted on the T-55 involved the PS-1 'Plavsredstva' (amphibious device). The PS-1 was tested with the T-55 and the BTS-2 armoured recovery tractor. The system was similar to earlier experiments conducted with the T-54 with aluminium pontoons, which were attached to the T-55 by locking points added to the base tank, with the 5.5 metric tonne pontoon set transported on land by two ZiL-157V tractor-trailer combinations. The PS-1 provided the T-55 with a forward speed of 14km/h and 8km/h in reverse should it be required, and a maximum speed on land of 25km/h for the limited time the combination would be so operated. The PS-1 experimental work later morphed into the PST-63 (Obiekt-619) 'Plavsredstva', also known as the PST-U, which was accepted for service with the Soviet Army, and the later-modified PST-63M, which was adapted for use with the current T-55A, T-62, T-64 and the earlier T-54.

T-55 WITH 'URAN' AND 'ALMAZ' TELEVISION CONTROL SYSTEM

The T-55 was used as a test-bed vehicle for both the 'Uran' and 'Almaz' television controls, both of which replaced the optical devices of the T-55 with television cameras linked to screens within the tank. Although both types were extensively tested on the T-55 and other tanks, such devices would not be adopted by the Soviet Army, reappearing on a production tank only with the T-14 'Armara' in the second decade of the 21st century.

(1) The T-55 afloat with the later PST-63 set. While the tank was a standard T-55, it required special fittings welded to the hull to clip on the pontoons for use.

(2) While bolted on, the fittings were much stronger than the normal engineer equipment mountings and were not interchangeable.

(3) The tank had relatively low freeboard when fitted and probably would have to rely on its OPVT equipment to prevent water ingress in all but very mild conditions.

(4) This tank is fitted with a PST wading set, but once ashore its mobility and ability to fight were extremely limited due to the pontoons, hence the system was immediately jettisoned on reaching shore.

(5) A comparison of three swimming vehicles: a T-55 with the PST-63 set; a T-54B with the PST-54 set; and a ZSU-57-2 with the PST-63 set.

(6) A T-55 being loaded onto a sectional pontoon bridge during a Soviet Army exercise in the 1960s.

CHAPTER FIVE
COMBAT USE OF THE T-55 TANK

As with its younger brother, the T-54, the T-55 enjoyed a long career in the Soviet Army and even into the early days of the reformed Russian Army. Under Soviet control the tank saw very little combat use or deployment, but it was widely exported to other nations. It was also joined by T-55 tanks of Czechoslovakian and Polish production, with the T-55 tank participating in many of the wars and combat operations from the mid 1960s to the present.

The results of most of those foreign operations showed that the T-55 was rarely, if ever, the dominant tank on the battlefield and more than a few times it was reduced to little more than a battlefield target. This was not due to any inherent failings of the T-55 itself, but mostly due to the fact that third-world customers – even with heavy Soviet training and advisor presence – were not able to employ the tanks effectively against their better-trained adversaries. This was very disappointing to the designers of the tank and evidently annoying to the Soviet military. Even today, Russian analysts note that their best tank designs such as the T-90A are of limited capability if the crew bails out and runs away the second the tank comes under fire.

The T-55 has been employed in so many different theatres and campaigns in the Middle East and Africa that there is no good way to cover all of them. Even today both sides are using the T-55 tank in the Syrian civil war as well as in the Kurds versus ISIS conflict in the northern part of Iraq, but overall numbers are unknown.

It should be noted that by the time most of the conflicts that are listed here took place, many of these user nations lumped T-54 and T-55 tanks together and deployed them as such, so precise numbers of losses are not possible to evaluate. Listed below are some of the better-known operations that the T-55 has participated in since its introduction into service nearly 60 years ago. The T-55 has had an impressively long service career, and continues in use around the world today.

THE SIX DAY WAR – JUNE 1967

Most of the Soviet-supplied tanks in this war used by the Arab armies were T-54s. There were a small number of T-55s in service as part of the armies of Egypt, Syria and Iraq, but only the Egyptian tanks undertook a major active role in the war. The Egyptians started with 950 T-54, T-55 and IS-3 tanks but suffered some heavy losses.

The Israeli Defence Forces (IDF) captured some 291 T-54A and 82 T-55 tanks from Egypt, and Syria lost 73 T-54 tanks during the war.

OPERATION *DUNAY* – AUGUST 1968

After the 'Czech Spring' in 1968 the Brezhnev government decided that the new government led by Alexander Dubček could not be permitted to break away from the Warsaw Pact and measures had to be taken to bring them back into the fold. As a result the Soviets planned and organized Operation *Dunay* (Danube) with the participation of several members of the Warsaw Pact.

On the night of 20 August 1968, 200,000 troops and up to 5,000 tanks (T-54, T-55, T-62 and one regiment of T-10M heavy tanks) belonging to the USSR, Poland, Hungary, Bulgaria and East Germany (the DDR) all invaded Czechoslovakia in a clear-cut move to quash the independence of the government. Generally, the Czechs offered only passive resistance to the invasion, so there was no confrontation with the invading forces. But there were three incidents involving T-55 tanks.

The worst of the three took place early in the invasion when the 6th Guards Tank Division and the 7th Guards Tank Division (GTD) – both equipped with a mixture of T-54 and T-55 tanks – ran into each other. The 6th had not painted their tanks with the invasion stripes as ordered while the 7th had done so, and thus when they saw the other tanks assumed they were Czechoslovakian resistance and engaged them, several tanks being destroyed before level heads intervened and stopped the shooting. The 7th GTD was sent back to Germany in disgrace and the 6th GTD presumably quickly added invasion stripes to their armour.

One side note not mentioned in many places was that when this was taking place, a US movie company was shooting the film *Bridge at Remagen* in the CSSR and using a large number of World War II-era American vehicles as movie props. One US vehicle column was shot on film as it raced to the bridge used in the movie to simulate the famous Rhine Bridge capture and ran head-on into a column of very much contemporary T-54 and T-55 tanks coming from the other direction. The Soviets had last heard that NATO and US 7th Army were heading toward the border due to the invasion, and thus for a few minutes the Soviets were ready to engage. Fortunately, somebody noted they were World War II-era vehicles with movie cameras deployed, and after a short discussion the Soviet tanks passed by.

The last incident happened on 21 August when a Bulgarian airborne unit arrived to secure Prague main airport. Two SU-85 (ASU-85) self-propelled guns were guarding the main road to the airport when they saw a tank roar out of a side road and head pell-mell for the entrance. Both self-propelled guns opened fire, and the result was that the tank blew up, with its turret flying through the air. The Bulgarians had heard the same news about the US 7th Army and thought they had destroyed an M48 – to their surprise they spotted the turret as being from a T-55. It had been the lead Soviet tank trying to link up with the Bulgarians. Needless to say, the Bulgarians were thanked for their 'internationalist' duty and sent back to Bulgaria under the watchful eyes of the Soviets.

SECOND INDO-PAKISTANI WAR (BANGLADESH LIBERATION WAR) – 1971

India and Pakistan had carried out numerous small clashes on their borders since 1947, with the first major war taking place in 1965. After that conflict, both sides began to rearm with new suppliers. Pakistan turned to China for its Type 59 tanks and India began purchasing T-54 and T-55 tanks from the Soviet Union. While the war was over quickly due to pressure from the US and the USSR, India effectively won the war and took nearly 90,000 Pakistani prisoners. Pakistan lost control of East Pakistan, which renamed itself Bangladesh, but the flood of refugees from that area caused serious social problems for the Indians in dealing with them.

Most of this war was fought in the air and at sea, so armour operations were not particularly significant. The Indians reportedly lost about 28 tanks and the Pakistanis about 68.

THE YOM KIPPUR WAR – OCTOBER 1973

After the military disaster of June 1967, the T-55 proved to be a 'best seller' to the Arab countries, with Egypt, Syria and Iraq buying large numbers of them from both the Soviets and Czechoslovakian and Polish models. But while their training improved from the woeful state of the June 1967 war, they still were not able to get the most out of the tanks and as a result lost huge numbers of them to the Israelis during the Yom Kippur War of 1973.

The worst of the losses took place on 6/7 October along the Golan Heights, when the Syrian 7th, 1st and 3rd Armoured Divisions with up to

900 tanks made a night attack on the defensive positions of the IDF. Theoretically as all of their tanks were fitted with infrared sights and searchlights – and the IDF had not been able to fit more than a handful of vehicles with these advantages, particularly none of the upgraded Centurions facing the Syrians – it should have been a resounding Syrian victory. It was not: the IDF managed to find a way to isolate the Syrian tanks, destroying a good number of them and forcing many others to be abandoned.

The Syrians and Iraqis lost some 1,500 tanks during the conflict, of which 260 were knocked out and the rest were abandoned. The Iraqi 3rd 'Saladin' Armoured Division was the sole Iraqi participant in the conflict but by the time it was committed massive IDF reinforcements had arrived and the unit lost 130 of its tanks against the Israelis in a matter of about 20 minutes. (Making the best of a bad situation, the Iraqis gave honour status to the 3rd as it had 'struck a blow' against the 'Zionist Entity' of Israel.)

The Egyptians fared somewhat better in regard to losses but still lost around 250 tanks to the Israelis, and without international pressure probably would have lost another 900 that were cut off by the IDF with the Egyptian 3rd Corps.

The IDF managed to obtain enough captured T-54, T-55 and T-62 tanks to rebuild them as the Tiran-4, Tiran-5 and Tiran-6 respectively and take them into service with the IDF as reserve vehicles. Later, after they were designated as obsolete, many T-54 and T-55 chassis were rebuilt as 'Achzarit' heavy armoured personnel carriers.

Israeli observations of the T-54/55 tanks were that they were a very tough opponent. To add to their problems, if the Syrians suffered a mobility kill they would 'play dead' and let the IDF tanks pass by and then turn their turrets to attack them, causing some casualties. The IDF soon adopted the tactic of firing into the Syrian tanks until either they visibly caught fire or the turret blew off to ensure they were knocked out.

However, unlike the 1967 war, this time the Soviet General Staff sent two observer teams down to determine what was going on and why the Arabs were suffering losses. One team was personally led by Kartsev (Egypt) and the other by P. I. Bazhenov (Syria). Kartsev took a slow route via Budapest to Cairo and in fact got to play tourist for a while as well.

Kartsev met with the head of the Egyptian Armoured Vehicle Directorate, General Kamal, both conversing in fluent English. They drove out to meet the head of Egyptian armour combat training, General Hosni, but they needed an Arabic translator for this officer. They eventually went to the front in the area of El-Kantara and viewed the results of the major battle that took place there, such as a knocked out IDF M48 Patton armed with a 105mm gun. Kartsev noted that most of their damage had been suffered from attacks by the 9M14 'Malyutka'

ATGM, which the Egyptians used in great numbers. The Egyptians noted they had lost 860 tanks of all types, and the IDF lost 690 tanks on the Sinai Peninsula.

The Egyptians also noted that the air-cooled engines in the American-built tanks were an advantage in the desert as they needed no water, but the Soviet-built tanks apparently held up well even with liquid-cooled engines. They also had the chance to visit and talk to both maintenance and restoration personnel. The teams returned to Moscow in December 1973 and made their evaluations. These operational and combat findings were used to improve the next generation of Soviet tanks – the T-64B, T-72 and T-80.

THE IRAN-IRAQ WAR – 1980–88

Iran and Iraq were uneasy neighbours due to both ethnic (Arab versus Persian) backgrounds and differing forms of Islam (Sunni versus Shiite). But under the Shah of Iran, relations were at least tolerable between that country and the Ba'athist government of Saddam Hussein in Iraq. However, with the fall of the Shah and emergence of the hard-line Shiite faction of the Ayatollah Khomeini in 1979, relations rapidly collapsed. Both sides wanted full control of the Shatt-al Arab waterway for oil exports; and with the fear of Iran sparking a Shiite revolt inside Iraq, Saddam attacked Iran on 22 September 1980.

Post 1991, several ex-Soviet countries, including the Russian Federation, Belarus and Ukraine rebuilt and modernized Soviet era inventory, primarily for export. Seen here, a modernized T-55AM in Kharkov, Tankman's Day 1997.

Ethiopian Army T-55A M-1965 during the Ogaden War, 1977.
Some of Ethiopian tanks were hastily overpainted in sand colour.
Quick identification yellow disks were applied on the turret sides,
glacis armour and hull rear plate. (Andrey Aksenov)

T-55A M-1969 from Tank Battalion of 101st Motor Rifle Regiment,
5th Guards Motor Rifle Division, Gerat province,
Afghanistan, 1982. (Andrey Aksenov)

The Iraqis started the war with around 2,700 tanks of all types and ended
it with 4,500 after considerable imports of replacement tanks. Most of them
were T-55s from all three producers and also Type 59 and Type 69-II tanks
from China (which the Iraqis simply called the 'Chinese T-55' and included
them in their T-55 strength totals). At the end they fielded a variety of T-54,

T-55, T-62, T-72, Type 59 and Type 69-II tanks.

The Iranians began with 1,740 M47, M60 and Chieftain tanks of which only 500 were in total considered functional, but ended up with around 1,000 as they had also purchased T-55 and Type 69-II tanks from second-hand stocks and from China.

OGADEN WAR - 1977-78

This war was fought between Somalia and Ethiopia for the Ogaden region. The Somalis used T-54 and T-55 tanks to defeat Ethiopian M41 and M47 tanks, but Ethiopia was later backed up by Cuban forces with T-62s. The Cubans quickly defeated the Somalis and drove them back into their territory.

UGANDAN-TANZANIAN WAR - 1978-79

Tanzania used its T-55s to inflict damage on the Ugandans who were fighting back with Sherman tanks.

AFGHANISTAN - DECEMBER 1979-FEBRUARY 1989

With the deposal of pro-Soviet President Taraki by new President Hafizullah Amin, the unstable situation in the Democratic Republic of Afghanistan (DRA) began to destabilize further, and the deteriorating situation in Afghanistan began to be considered a threat to the Southern Republics of the Soviet Union. After much deliberation, and against much military advice, the decision was taken to send troops into the country. In December 1979, Soviet airborne and land forces entered the country. Soviet forces took over all military bases in the country and either took control of Afghan weaponry or disabled it to prevent further use. Not for the first time in the history of Afghanistan, foreign occupiers, in this case the Soviet Union, faced a protracted and brutal war of attrition in the country.

The DRA Army was equipped with T-54, T-55 and T-62 tanks, so using them alongside Soviet forces was not a problem for the new 40th Army, as the group of Soviet forces in Afghanistan became known. Most of the Soviet tanks used in Afghanistan were T-62s; they had replaced most of the T-55s in the nearest units to the border, and testing of the newer T-64 and T-72 tanks found their narrower power band and 7-speed transmissions tired out driver-mechanics in mountainous conditions. The DRA made the most of its use of their T-55 and T-62 tanks as their lower powered (but wider power band) engines and 5-speed transmissions were better suited to mountainous terrain.

Both sides used the T-55 as mobile artillery rather than as tanks, it being found that in most places the guns could not elevate far enough to employ them in a direct fire mode against enemy positions high on the sides of the mountains or in narrow passes.

While the Soviet Union listed 147 T-62 tanks lost, there is no accurate listing of T-55 losses by the DRA. Many that broke down in place were still used as firing positions or pillboxes for years after the Soviet Army departed the country.

WESTERN SAHARA CONFLICT – 1980–82

The Polisario movement fought against the Moroccan government but received aid and weapons from Libya. They were able to use up to 60 T-54 and T-55 tanks at a time, such as on 12 October 1981, when they attacked and destroyed a 2,600-man Moroccan garrison, losing only five tanks in the process. Later they used them for raids on government outposts.

OPERATION *PEACE FOR GALILEE* – 1982

After considerable Syrian provocation and a civil war in Lebanon, the IDF entered the country to stop the war and drive out the Syrian forces provoking and backing the conflict. At that time the Syrians had rebuilt their tank forces to around 2,200 T-54 and T-55 tanks as well as 1,100 T-62 and 400 T-72 tanks. The PLO (Palestine Liberation Organization) also had some tanks, including approximately 40–50 T-54/T-55 types given to them by the Syrians.

The IDF had around 1,100 tanks on the Syrian front of which 250 were T-54 or T-55 types, and 150 were T-62s, but they increased the force to about 1,200 from reserves. While the war was essentially inconclusive (although Syria did curtail many of its operations in Lebanon after the war), the Syrians again lost about 30 per cent of their tanks to the IDF.

SRI LANKAN CIVIL WAR – 1983–2009

During the Sri Lankan Civil War, the government fought to suppress the rebel Tamil Tigers. In 1995 the combat advantage switched over to the government, who used their T-55 tanks to take the initiative.

LIBYA-CHAD WAR – 1987

Probably the most embarrassing event in the (non) combat history of the T-55 took place in May 1987, when Chadian forces using pickup trucks armed with

(1) This Polish-built T-55 with the 'Engima' arrays is at the Bovington Tank Museum and bears the 'zap' marks placed on it by British forces during the Gulf War.

(2) The Bovington tank has its driver-mechanic's foremost section elevated and cut open to show how the array is fitted inside the sheet metal casing.

(3) Another view, showing how wide the array opens for driver-mechanic access.

(4) Unlike its APG sister, this tank did have its light assembly reattached to the right glacis panel, but it was damaged at some point.

(5) Short arrays were attached to the fenders to protect the fuel tanks.

(6) Eight arrays were attached to each side and were 'stepped' towards the end to permit the tank to depress its gun in its frontal arc of fire as needed.

(7) While the fender is braced to support the armour, the forward rear fuel tank is missing.

(8) The rear array on the Bovington tank.

(9) It also has the stowage bin between the support arms. Apparently the 'zap' artists on this tank were fans of the US comic strip 'Calvin & Hobbes'!

(10) A close-up, showing how massive the braces and arms are that hold the rear array in place.

(11) There is a close fit between the side armour arrays and the turret arrays, leaving little space for a high-explosive anti-tank projectile or ATGM to get past them.

(12) At the 1991 Association of the US Army convention, one of the side arrays was presented after its removal from the sheet metal container. It consisted of a combination of steel, rubber and aluminium plates spaced apart inside the container. To the shock of Western experts, it was found to provide effective protection against all anti-tank missiles with the possible exception of the US Hellfire missile.

machine guns stormed the massive Libyan base at Ouadi Doum in Chad at night and caused the panicked Libyans to either run away or surrender. All of their tanks at the base (noted as up to 200 armoured vehicles in total) were captured intact without even a pretence at defence. Over the course of the war Chad destroyed 183 and captured 113 T-55 tanks from Libya.

ANGOLAN CIVIL WAR – MID 1970s TO 1987

T-55s were used during the ongoing conflicts in the country by Angolan and Cuban forces at different times. Republic of South Africa (RSA) forces with Ratel armoured cars managed to defeat them, but only with difficulty.

GULF WAR – AUGUST 1990–FEBRUARY 1991

On 2 August 1990 Saddam Hussein ordered his forces to take back the '19th Province' of Iraq, as he referred to the country of Kuwait. The Kuwaitis were unable to defend themselves, and in less than 24 hours the Iraqis had occupied all of Kuwait. The UN demanded they leave the country but was ignored by Saddam Hussein and over the course of the next five months a 35-nation coalition of forces led by the US was built up to force Saddam to leave the sheikdom.

At that time, Saddam Hussein had up to 5,500 tanks of all types in seven corps and the Republican Guards, with 54 divisions in the regular army and 12 Republican Guards divisions. All but some specialized infantry and commando units had large numbers of tanks assigned. The tanks used by the Iraqis included the T-54, T-55 (all types), Type 59, Type 69-II, T-62, T-72, T-72M and T-72M1 types. The T-54, T-55, and Chinese tanks were all lumped together and used in nearly interchangeable fashion (the Type 69-II was referred to as the 'Chinese T-55' in official Iraqi documents), so it is not possible to definitively sort out their numbers.

The Iraqis were no fools, having fought the Iranians for eight years, and were adept at moving their tanks around in the dark, but this could cause problems. On 29 January 1990 the 5th Mechanized Division and 3rd 'Saladin' Armoured Division changed places on the battlefield, with mixed results. The 3rd had a brigade of T-62s run into US Marines and suffered casualties; the 5th drove into the city of Al-Khafji and engaged Saudi units in the centre of the city. As the T-55s had their turrets reversed, the Saudis thought they were surrendering; however, it was an administrative move, as the turrets were

(1) One of the most intriguing foreign modifications to the T-55 was the Iraqi passive armour array dubbed 'Engima' in the West. The package was fitted to both Soviet- and Polish-built T-55s as well as Chinese Type 69-II tanks, and was identical for all three types. This one is displayed by the 203rd MI Battalion at Aberdeen Proving Ground, Maryland.
(2) The armour arrays cover the glacis, turret front, turret rear, and sides of the tank.
(3) Holes were cut in the arrays for the tow hooks on the front of the glacis; no panels were fitted to the lower glacis.

(4) The rear of the turret was protected by a larger rectangular box, with a small bin for kit and equipment between its support arms.
(5) There is nothing fitted directly to the turret rear to provide protection.
(6) The armour arrays were attached on hinges for examining parts of the tank during general inspection.
(7) To support the side arrays, the fenders were given extra bracing to carry the weight.

(8) This Polish-built T-55 shows the fact that the direct fire sight and machine gun port were left unprotected.

(9) The Iraqis also fitted light armoured covers over the main and commander's searchlights to protect them from artillery fragments.

(10) In order for the driver-mechanic to access his hatch, the section of armour over his hatch was spring-loaded so he could lift it out of the way and lock it in place until needed.

(11) Another view of the fender bracing and attachment of the side armour arrays.

(12) The standard AA MG mount received no protection.

(13) Likewise, the hull rear area also had no protection from the new arrays.

(14) A side view, showing that the armour arrays, as is correct, provide protection primarily for the forward 60° arc of fire on the vehicle, the direction most common in tank versus tank combat.

reversed to give the driver-mechanics more visibility. The Iraqis dropped down into the tanks, swivelled the turrets around and began firing. The Saudis later claimed they had used deception, but this was not the case. Eventually US forces and Qatari tankers in AMX-30 tanks drove the T-55s out of the city.

What is known is that when the ground war finally broke out in late February, more than 1,860 Iraqi armoured vehicles were destroyed in action and still others captured. One T-55 was noted as destroyed by a British Challenger II at nearly 3,000 metres, so their survivability on the battlefield against latest-generation Western tanks was not high. But most of these losses were due to the lack of skills among Iraqi tankers coupled with a lack of modern thermal sights and ammunition.

While the USAF (United States Air Force) in particular claimed a large number of tanks killed from the air (up to the total number of tanks deployed by the Iraqi Army), ground observation showed that the majority of destroyed tanks were actually destroyed by either Hellfire or TOW missiles from attack helicopters and Bradley IFVs, or kinetic ammunition from Coalition tanks.

Many of the Iraqi T-55s showed signs of having been upgraded from Model 1958 status to Model 1969 status by a retrofitted loader's cupola with 12.7mm DShKM machine gun mount.

One unique Iraqi tank modification was encountered during *Desert Storm* – a number of T-55 and Type 69-II tanks fitted with a passive armour array. As it puzzled Western analysts and military experts at first, the new design was dubbed the T-55 'Engima'. Several were captured during the war and it was found they used any type of T-55 related chassis – Soviet, Polish or Czech T-55s, or Type 69-II tanks.

The array protected the frontal 60° arc of the tank and also the rear of the turret. While laughed at as crude, when the armour segments were removed and examined it was found they were filled with stacked plates of spaced steel and rubber sheet. To the shock of the experts, subsequent tests showed that the 'Heath Robinson' armour of the T-55 Engima tanks would defeat all Western anti-tank missiles and handheld anti-tank means except the Hellfire. But only a relative handful of tanks were so equipped, apparently mostly command vehicles.

NAGORNO-KARABAKH – 1991–94

This was another war fought by former states of the USSR between Azerbaijan and the breakaway region of Nagorno-Karabakh. The Azeris used T-55s at one point in the conflict.

TRANSDNIESTER CONFLICT - 1991

The Moldovans used T-55s against this breakaway territory, but they apparently were not a decisive force in the conflict.

OPERATION *IRAQI FREEDOM* - MARCH-APRIL 2003

The Iraqi Army still had a good number of T-54/T-55 and Type 69-II tanks surviving after the first Gulf War In 1991. Their totals were estimated at between 2,200 and 2,600 of all types. However, in this conflict few of them took part in combat operations. This appears to be mostly due to a strategy by the Iraqis of simply limiting resistance to where they could inflict damage on the Coalition forces and then fading into the population to conduct an ongoing guerrilla war as 'fighters'.

The Iraqis still had 16 regular army divisions and two smaller Republican Guards corps of three divisions each, but they were overmatched by Coalition forces. They either abandoned their heavy weapons when confronted by superior forces or were easily brushed aside in the course of the 21-day war.

SYRIAN CIVIL WAR - 2011 TO THE PRESENT

Prior to the start of the current War In Syria, the government had around 5,000 tanks, of which around 2,000 were T-54/T-55 types. But most of these were in reserve and not in very good shape. Since the start of combat they have been captured by various factions and used against either the government or each other when they can be made to operate.

Currently the Syrian government has around 3,300 tanks under its control, but most of these are later T-62, T-72 and T-90 types, with both T-72B3 and T-90A also being recently provided by Russia. It is not known with any accuracy how many T-54/T-55 tanks remain in rebel or ISIS hands.

APPENDICES

APPENDIX ONE
T-55/T-55A TANK PRODUCTION BY YEAR

Plant No. 174 Omsk	Total
1958	610
1959	1,802
1960	2,267
1961	2,295
1962	1,696
1963	740
1964	570
1965	470
1966	686
1967	712
1968	1,064
Total at Omsk 1958–68	12,912
Total at Plant No. 75 Kharkov 1968–79; and Plant No. 183 Nizhny Tagil 1973–79 (annual production from each unknown)	11,000 (estimated)
Grand Total	23,000+

Romanian Army T-55A during Revolution events, Timişoara, December 1989. (Andrey Aksenov)

APPENDIX TWO
T-54/T-55 IN SOVIET SERVICE AS OF 1 NOVEMBER 1990 PER CONVENTIONAL FORCES IN EUROPE CFE

(Area covered is west of the Ural Mountains and includes the Groups of Forces as defined in Note 1)

Type	Cat I	Cat II	Cat III	Cat IV	Cat V	Total
T-54 Mod 51	0	250	248	0	25	523
T-54K	1	1	0	0	0	2
T-54B	901	296	244	0	330	1,771
T-54BK	24	16	10	0	8	58
T-54M	642	243	31	0	167	1,083
T-54MK	26	8	3	0	68	105
Total T-54	1,594	814	536	0	598	3,542
T-55	468	301	231	0	167	1,167
T-55K	74	6	5	0	68	153
T-55A	877	709	477	0	168	2,231
T-55AD	237	177	176	0	60	650
T-55AK	80	72	20	0	8	180
T-55AM	0	0	79	0	67	146
T-55AMD	21	21	21	0	0	63
T-55AMK	1	1	1	0	0	3
T-55AM	39	39	36	0	0	114
T-55M	1,006	496	342	0	517	2,361
T-55MK	0	18	13	0	2	33
T-55MV	143	143	115	0	0	401
T-55MVK	2	2	2	0	0	6
Total T-55	2,948	1,985	1,518	0	1,057	8,565
Total T-54 / T-55	4,542	2,799	2,054	0	1,655	12,107

Note 1: The categories listed are Soviet operational readiness status indicators. They are defined as follows:

I – Fully combat ready
II – Mostly combat ready but needs servicing
III – Likely combat ready but needs repairs
IV – Not combat ready and needs major repairs or rebuilding
V – Inoperative and needs either complete rebuilding or scrapping

Note 2: This is only the part of the Soviet Union that was west of the Ural Mountains; more tanks were stored in depots east of the Urals not counted under the Conventional Forces in Europe (CFE) treaty or were in service with units in the eastern military districts.

APPENDIX THREE
T-54 AND T-55 TANKS REBUILT BETWEEN 1985 AND 1990

Year	T-54	T-55
1985	69	131
1986	60	126
1987	80	103
1988	44	96
1989	30	129
1990	89	108
Total	372	693

APPENDIX FOUR
RELATED IZDELIYE/OBIEKT NUMBER FOR T-55 TANK DESIGNS

Article Number	FactoryNumber	Vehicle and Description
137G2	183	Prototype of the T-55 tank
155	183, 75, 174	T-55 Model 1958
155K	183	T-55K commander's tank
155A	183, 75, 174	T-55A Model 1961
155AK	174	T-55AK commander's tank
155M	Rebuild	T-55 rebuilt and modernized tank – 1983
155AM	Rebuild	T-55A rebuilt and modernized tank – 1983
155MK	Rebuild	T-55K rebuilt and modernized tank – 1983
155AMK	Rebuild	T-55AK rebuilt and modernized tank – 1983
155M-1	Rebuild	T-55M with V-46-5 engine as rebuilt and modernized – 1983
155AM-1	Rebuild	T-55AM with V-46-5 engine as rebuilt and modernized – 1983
155AD	Upgrade	T-55M fitted with the 'Drozd' active protective system – 1983
155AMD	Rebuild	T-55AM fitted with the 'Drozd' active protective system – 1983
155MV	Rebuild	T-55M fitted with 'Kontakt-1' explosive reactive armour (ERA) bricks
155AMV	Rebuild	T-55AM fitted with 'Kontakt-1' explosive reactive armour (ERA) bricks
482	75	TO-55 tank fitted with ATO-200 flamethrower as a co-axial weapons system
602	174	MTU-55 tank bridge-layer
604	174	TMT jet-propelled mine sweeper
605	174	T-55 with new electrical system to be tested for a future tank project
606	174	T-55 with an automatic transmission
607	174	Initial designator for Omsk-built T-55A tanks – later redesignated 155A
615	174	Initial object number for the T-55AK – later redesignated as 155AK
616	174	IMR engineer obstacle clearing vehicle
625	174	T-55A fitted with three 9M14 'Malyutka' ATGM launcher

APPENDIX FIVE
TECHNICAL CHARACTERISTICS

Technical characteristic	T-55 Model 1958	T-55A Model 1961	T-55 Model 1969	T-55M Model 1983	T-55AM Model 1983
General data					
Year produced	1958	1963	1969	1983	1983
Combat weight metric tonnes	36–36.5	37.5	36.5	40.9	41.5
Crewmen	4	4	4	4	4
Overall dimensions in mm					
Overall over gun	9,000	9,000	9,000	9,000	9,000
Length (hull)	6,040	6,040	6,040	6,040	6,040
Width (over skirts)	3,270	3,270	3,270	3,526	3,526
Height (top of turret)	2,350	2,350	2,350	2,350	2,350
Power to weight ratio (hp/tonne)	16.1				
Ground clearance in mm	425	425	425	392	392
Armament					
Type of gun/number	D-10T2S	D-10T2S	D-10T2S	D-10T2S	D-10T2S
Calibre in mm	100	100	100	100	100
Length of barrel in mm (calibres)	5600 L/56				
Aiming limits (degrees)					
Traverse	360	360	360	360	360
Elevation	+18 to -5	+18 to -5	+18 to -5	+18 to -5	+18 to -5
Muzzle velocity in m/s	600	–	600	600	600
Weight of projectile in kg	15.6	–	–	–	–
Maximum range	4,000m	–	–	–	–
AP	895/15.88	895/15.88	895/15.88	895/15.88	895/15.88
AP penetration/1000m	185mm	185mm	185mm	185mm	185mm
APDS	–	–	–	?	?
APDS penetration/2000m	–	–	–	275mm	275mm
HEAT	–	–	–	?	?
HEAT penetration/any	–	–	–	390mm	390mm
Anti-tank Guided Missile	–	–	–	9K116 Bastion	9K116 Bastion 500
RHA penetration (mm)				500	
Co-axial machine gun number	1	1	1	1	1
Calibre (mm)	7.62	7.62	7.62	7.62	7.62
Type	SGMT	SGMT	SGMT	PKT	PKT
Bow machine gun number	1 (bow)		1 (bow)		
Calibre (mm)	7.62	None	7.62	None	None
Type	SGMT		SGMT		
Anti-aircraft machine gun number			1	1	1
Calibre (mm)	None	None	12.7	12.7	12.7
Type			DShK/ DShKM	DShKM	DShKM
Basic load					
Main gun	43	43	43	43	43
7.62mm	3500	2750	3500	3500	3500
12.7mm	–	–	300	300	300
Armament stabilizer	STP-2 Tsiklon	STP-2 Tsiklon	STP-2 Tsiklon	Tsiklon-M1	Tsiklon-M1

Rangefinder	-	-	-	KTD-2	KTD-2
Gunner's primary sight	TSh-2B-22	TSh-32	TSh-32	TShSM-32	TShSM-32
Gunner's night sight	TPN-1	TPN-1	TPN-1	TPN-1	TPN-1
Gunner's missile sight	-	-	-	1K13	1K13
Armour protection (thickness/angle of inclination from the vertical in degrees)					
Hull mm/degrees Glacis					
Upper	100/60	100/60	100/60	100/60+200	100/60+200
Lower	100/55	100/55	100/55	100/55	100/55
Sides	80/0	80/0	80/0	80/0	80/0
Screen	None	None	None	None	None
Rear:					
Upper	45/60	45/60	45/60	45/60	45/60
Centre	45/17	45/17	45/17	45/17	45/17
Lower	30/70	30/70	30/70	30/70	30/70
Roof	30/90; 20/90	30/90; 20/90	30/90; 20/90	30/90; 20/90	30/90; 20/90
Hull floor	20/90	20/90	20/90	20/90 +80 spaced	20/90 +80 spaced
Turret mm/degrees					
Mantlet	n/a	n/a	n/a	n/a	n/a
Glacis	200/0	200-108/0-60	200-108/0-60	200-108/0-60 +290 160-86/0-60	200-108/0-60 +290 160-86/0-60
Sides	160-125/0-45	160-86/0-60	160-86/0-60 136-100/0-45 65-48/0-45	136-100/0-45 65-48/0-45	136-100/0-45 65-48/0-45
Rear	n/a	n/a	n/a	n/a	n/a
Top	30/81	n/a	n/a	n/a	n/a
Armour thickness (tabular)					
Hull mm/degrees glacis					
Upper	200	200	200	400+	400+
Lower	175	175	175	175	175
Sides	80	80	80	80+	80+
Screens	None	None	None	None	None
Rear					
Upper	90	90	90	90	90
Middle	45	45	45	45	45
Lower	88	88	88	88	88
Roof	30; 20	30; 20	30; 20	30; 20	30; 20
Hull floor	20	20	20	20+	20+80
Turret, mm/degrees					
Mantlet	n/a	n/a	n/a	n/a	n/a
Glacis	200	200-216	200-216	490-516+	490-516+
Sides	160-179	160-172	160-172;136-143	160-172;136-143	160-172;136-143
Rear	n/a	n/a	65-60	65-60	65-60
Top	30	n/a	n/a	n/a	n/a
Communications equipment					
Primary radio set	R-113	R-113	R-123	R-173	R-173
Intercom system	R-120	R-120	R-124	R-174	R-174
Command set (K models)	R-112	R-112	R-112	R-134	R-134
Primary antenna	1, 3, or 4 metre whip	1, 3, or 4 metre whip	1, 3, or 4 metre whip	1, 3, or 4 metre whip	1, 3, or 4 metre whip
Fixed antenna (K models)	10 metre	10 metre	10 metre	10 metre	10 metre
Mobility					
Top speed (km/h)	50	50	50	54	54

Obstacle negotiation					
Grade in degrees	30	30	30	30	30
Slope in degrees	30	30	30	30	30
Wall in metres	0.73	0.73	0.73	0.73	0.73
Ford in metres/with OPVT	1.4/5	1.4/5	1.4/5	1.4/5	1.4/5
Trench in metres	2.7	2.7	2.7	2.7	2.7
Average ground pressure (kg/cm2)	0.93	0.82	0.82	0.92	0.93
Highway range in kilometres					
Base	485–500	485–500	485–500	485–500	485–500
With auxiliary tanks	650–715	650–715	650–715	650–715	650–715
Fuel capacity in litres	680+285 (400 Aux)	680+285 (400 Aux)	680+285 (400 Aux)	680+285 (400 Aux)	680+285 (400 Aux)
Engine-transmission installation					
Engine – type	V-55	V-55	V-55	V-55U or V-46-5M	V-55U or V-46-5M
Type	Diesel liquid cooled				
Cycles	4				
Number of cylinders	12				
Layout	60 V type				
Cylinder bore (mm)	150				
Piston stroke (mm)	180; 186.7				
Maximum power (hp)	580	580	580	640 or 690	640 or 690
RPM at maximum power	2,000				
Displacement in litres	38.88				
Transmission type	Mechanical				
Torque converter	No				
Gearbox type	Simple, mechanical				
Number of speeds fwd/rev	5/1				
Steering gear	Planetary	Planetary	Planetary	Planetary	Planetary
Running gear					
Suspension type	Individual torsion bar				
Shock absorbers	4	4	4	4	4
Track drive	Drive wheels located at rear of hull				
Length of run on ground (mm)	3,840	3,840	3,840	3,840	3,840
Track width (mm)	580	580	580	580	580
Track pitch (mm)	137	137	137	137	137
Number of links	90	90	90	91	91
Type of Track	OMSh metal hinged	OMSh metal hinged	OMSh metal hinged	RMSh rubber bushed	RMSh rubber bushed
Number of road wheels per side	5	5	5	5	5
Road wheels (mm) (D – diameter, W – width)	810 D 165 W	810 D 165 W	810 D 165 W	810 D 165 W	810 D 165 W
Road wheel tyres	Attached				
Number of return rollers	None				

Note: late production T-55A tanks were (from 1969) also fitted with the 12.7mm DShKM machine gun and carried 300 rounds of 12.7mm ammunition for that weapon. Rebuilt tanks carry either the NSVT 'Utes' or 6P7 'Kord' machine gun if available. Command tanks were also not fitted with a bow machine gun.

APPENDIX SIX
KNOWN CLIENT USERS OF THE T-55 MEDIUM TANK

While most of the foreign clients that purchased or were given T-54 tanks also received T-55 tanks at a later date, many of them also rolled the two types together and counted them among the same tank totals. This also included those obtained from Poland and Czechoslovakia, and only close examination of the tanks for either their serial numbers or minor design characteristics would enable Soviet, Czech or Polish tanks to be differentiated.

BELOW LEFT The official CSE portrait of a Czech T-55A tank as provided to the co-ordinating committee. Handbooks were issued with these photos for counting purposes by NATO personnel.
BOTTOM LEFT The CSE side view of a Czech T-55AM2B in 1990. The added 'Kladivo' sensor mast and laser range finder are visible in this view.
BELOW RIGHT Rear view of the T-55AM2B, with the Czech redesigned engine deck and covers and modified ZIP bins on the fenders. Note that it retains the older two-section snorkel above the unditching log.
BOTTOM RIGHT Front view of the T-55AM2B. This tank has the complete BDD armour package and 9M116/1K13 'Bastion' sight and fire control system, as well as modified headlights due to the glacis appliqué armour.

Early Soviet production tanks usually had a date of YYMM (year/month) followed by a letter followed by a one-up monthly or summary production number of the vehicle. For example, 5411V107 would be a UVZ-built T-54 Model 1951 built in November 1954; 5006E150 was a Kharkov built T-54 Model 1949 built in June 1950. In 1970 the codes were changed to a letter for the year, two digits for the month of production and a two-letter code for the manufacturing plant followed by the one-up number. G11GT2432 is an Omsk-built T-55 produced in November 1977. The early codes were Cyrillic B (English V) for UVZ, E for Kharkov, and Cyrillic Г (G) for Omsk; when the system changed the codes became VT for the UVZ (V = UVZ, T = tank), ET for Kharkov, and GT for Omsk.

After 1970, here are the year codes used:

A preserved T-55 AM2B at the Czech Republic Armoured Museum in Lesany.

Year	Letter (Cyrllic-English)
1970	Л – L
1971	Н – N
1972	П – P
1973	М – M
1974	Р – R
1975	А – A
1976	Д – D
1977	Г – G
1978	Б – B
1979	В – V

ABOVE LEFT The same T-55 AM2B at the Czech Republic Armoured Museum in Lesany, 1998.
ABOVE RIGHT An ex-East German NVA T-55 at the Muckleburgh Collection, Norfolk, England, now reflagged as a 'Soviet' tank. This tank was of Polish manufacture. (Peter Plume)

Here are the known T-54/T-55-using countries and estimated numbers of vehicles on hand and used over the years.

Country	Number	Remarks
Abkhazia	100	Total tanks – number operational not known
Afghanistan	1.005	Ordered from the USSR from ex-Soviet stocks. Delivered in a batch of 50 and a batch of 200 T-54s and the rest T-55s
Albania	75	T-54s from the USSR – now out of service
Algeria	435	165 T-54 and 270 T-55 ordered from the USSR
Angola	350+	Mixed batch of T-54 and T-55 tanks, later supplemented by ex-Czech and Polish tanks
Armenia	5	Obtained from Georgia
Azerbaijan	95	T-55 tanks plus derivative vehicles
Bangladesh	15	Ex-Egyptian tanks
Belarus	29	T-55 tanks – out of service
Bosnia and Herzegovina	162	T-54/T-55 – accumulated by various sources over the years
Bulgaria	1,800	Ordered from the USSR – most now out of service
Cambodia	215	100 T-54 and 115 T-55 ordered from the USSR in 1989 and 1990
Central African Republic	3	As of 2017
Chad	60	Many captured from Libya
Chile	4	Captured Syrian tanks ordered from Israel for familiarization
Côte d'Ivoire	10	As of 2017
Croatia	186	Inherited from Yugoslavia – used in wars with the Serbs
CSSR	2,700*	Some purchased from the USSR but most domestically produced
Cuba	1,300	T-55 provided from the USSR 1963–1975
Czech Republic	6	Armoured recovery vehicles only
DDR (East Germany)	1,725	202 ordered from the USSR; 488 more T-54A and T-54AM tanks of Polish manufacture purchased at a later date; total of 1,725 T-54/T-55 tanks of all types at reunification in 1989
Democratic Republic of the Congo	32	Accumulated from various sources over the years
Republic of the Congo	<25	Mixed hand-me-down collection of T-54 and T-55 tanks
DPRK	1,100	T-55 tanks ordered from the USSR in two groups and possibly supplemented by locally built tanks
Egypt	840	Ordered from 1961 – many of Czech manufacture; now in storage
Equatorial Guinea	3	As of 2017
Eritrea	<270	As of 2012
Ethiopia	1,146	246 T-54 and 900 T-55 ordered in 1977, 1980–88
Finland	170	Ordered from the USSR in 1960, 1965 and 1967
Georgia	120(-)	Mixed order of T-54s and T-55AM2 tanks from Czech Republic
Guinea	8	8 T-54s ordered in 1974 from the USSR
Hungary	800	T-54/T-55 tanks provided in 1964 and 1965
India	1,850	300 T-54 ordered from the USSR in 1954, with follow-on orders of T-55 and supplemented by 274 Czechoslovakian-built T-54 tanks
Indonesia	?	Mostly recovery vehicles based on the T-55
Iran	<540	T-54, T-55 and Chinese Type 59 tanks counted together
Iraq	1,400	1,000 Soviet T-55s and 400 Czechoslovakian tanks from 1958 onward
Israel	1,500(-)	Captured tanks from the 1967 and 1973 wars – rebuilt first as Ti-67 tanks and then as Tiran 4 tanks (mixed T-54 and T-55 tank types), most now scrapped
Kazakhstan	540	T-54/T-55 but operation status unknown
Kurdistan	?	About 250 ex-Iraqi Army T-54, T-55 and Type 69 tanks in service
Laos	15	Ordered from the USSR in 1973
Latvia	3	As of 2017
Lebanon	180(-)	Ordered from Syria in 1991 – ex-Soviet tanks
Lesotho	1	As of 2017
Libya	2,250	Ordered from the USSR in three batches – 1970, 1975, and 1976

Mali	12	T-54s still in service
Mauretania	<35	T-55 and some recovery vehicles on T-55 chassis
Mongolia	<370	Ordered from the USSR in 1961–64
Morocco	40	Ordered from the USSR in 1960 (T-54B) and later supplemented by 80 T-54 tanks from Czechoslovakian production
Mozambique	110	Ordered from the USSR in 1983–85
Myanmar (Burma)	10	As of 2017
Namibia	?	Some as of 2017
Nicaragua	127	Ordered from the USSR and Czechoslovakia in 1984; 65 now in storage
Nigeria	100	As of 2017
Pakistan	100	Ordered from the USSR in 1968
Peru	280	Ordered from the USSR in 1973 – now mostly in storage and inoperative
Poland	3,000*	Some from the USSR but most tanks of domestic production – some later upgraded to T-54AM standards
Romania	1,786	Mixture of T-54, T-55 and Romanian TR-85/TR-580 T-55-built variants
Russia	2,800	T-54/T-55 in storage and awaiting scrapping
Rwanda	24	Mixed stocks of T-54 and T-55 tanks
Serbia and Montenegro	1,980	Remaining from former Yugoslavia (apparently total supplied during 1962–70 when still Yugoslavia – many to breakaway republics)
Slovakia	?	Some as of 2017
Somalia	135	100 ordered from the USSR in 1972 and 35 purchased from Egypt in 1977
South Ossetia	12	T-55 as of 2008
South Sudan	?	As of 2017
Sri Lanka	62	T-55/T-55AM2 tanks plus 18 recovery vehicles
Sudan	<350	T-54/55 ordered from the USSR in 1969
Syria	2,250	Ordered from the USSR in 1958, 1967 and 1978, many now in storage
Tanzania	32	Ordered from East Germany in 1979
Togo	2	Ordered from Egypt
Uganda	<185	Ordered from the USSR in 1974
Ukraine	20	Remaining; balance of 1,200 held in 1990 which were sold or scrapped
Uruguay	15	Ex-IDF Ti-67 rebuilds
USA	11	Former East German NVA tanks
SRV	850	Roughly 250 provided pre-1973, 600 T-55 1973–75
Yemen	450	T-54 and T-55 from various sources
North Yemen	100	T-54/T-55 received in 1979–80
Yugoslavia	160	Ordered from the USSR – migrated to subsequent independent countries
Zambia	5	Ordered from the USSR in 1975
Zimbabwe	20	Ordered from the USSR in 1984

*Note : The CSSR (Czechoslovakia) and Poland were licensed producers of the T-54 and made a number of modifications to their models that differentiated them from Soviet tanks. Plus signs mean more than that number is likely, minus signs that they are part of a mixed reporting of T-54 and T-55 tanks. Many of the tanks were lost or destroyed in various conflicts and most of the numbers presented here only indicate their initial known holdings. Also captured tanks may be listed with their new owners, and others handed down to other countries, so numbers for one country may migrate to another. Other countries like Iraq also counted Chinese Type 59 and Type 69-II tanks as 'T-55s' in their armies.

ABOVE The official CSE portrait of a Hungarian T-55A of Czech production.
ABOVE RIGHT Rear view of the same tank, showing the modifications to the engine deck and extra stowage bins added to the fenders of the tank, as well as the radiation-clad loader's hatch.
RIGHT A Hungarian T-55AM2B tank of Czech production, showing the 'Kladivo' mast folded and the laser range finder in place. The AAMG and its mount have been removed.
BELOW Front view of the same Hungarian T-55AM2B, showing a different (actually original) headlight assembly, now moved on top of the glacis appliqué.
BOTTOM CFE portrait of a Polish T-55, with all equipment except the storage tarpaulin in place.

TOP LEFT Front view of the same tank, showing the unique Polish marker device on the front left fender, stowage bins, and the oval Czech and Polish OPVT cover for the telescopic sight in place.

TOP RIGHT Rear view of the tank, with the modified engine deck and also a different location for stowage of the two-section snorkel.

ABOVE LEFT A Polish T-55 during an exercise and fitted with the BTU-55 bulldozer blade assembly.

ABOVE A Polish T-55 tank on exercise in Poland when the country was in the Warsaw Pact.

LEFT A Polish-built T-55AM2P tank preserved along with a T-55 at Fort IX, Warsaw, Poland.

BOTTOM The CFE portrait of a Romanian Army T-55A from 1990. By this time their TR-580 modified T-55 tanks had been retired.

ABOVE Rear view of the Romanian Army T-55A, showing it to be a Soviet-built model. Again, note the stowage for the two-section OPVT snorkel at the rear.

ABOVE RIGHT A Romanian Soviet-built T-55AM2 tank at the Romanian National Military Museum in Bucharest, 2012.

RIGHT A T-55A tank at the Great Patriotic War Memorial Museum, Kiev (now Kyiv).

BELOW Another Ukrainian T-55A tank, at the Kiev (Kyiv) Tank School in Ukraine. This one shows one of the stowage locations for the later three-section snorkel.

APPENDIX SEVEN
SOVIET STANDARDIZED LIFE CYCLE FOR ARMOURED VEHICLES

All Soviet tank designs began with a recognized need for a certain class of combat vehicle. This would be assigned as a project, often with a codename.

1 All new projects started with a request from the Council of Ministers of the USSR (SM SSSR) and the Central Committee (TsK). These were given to the relevant design and production facilities who then decided if they could meet the project requirements. If they could, they were tasked with carrying out scientific research work on a project to determine its viability.

2 **Scientific Design Work** (Nauchno-Issledivatal'naya Rabota or NIR). This was, and remains today, the scientific work that would determine the feasibility of a project and lay out possible solutions to the tasking. At this stage the project was either given a project name (e.g. 'Liven'<th>', 'Oka', 'Akatsiya', etc.) or a manufacturing plant internal designator. Once the NIR work was approved by the Scientific Committee for the Council of Ministers, the manufacturing plant was then authorized to carry out prototype design work.

3 **Prototype Design Work** (Opytno-Konstruktorskaya Rabota or OKR). At this stage, the project was given an article designator or Obiekt number (e.g. Obiekt-137G2, Obiekt-482). This stage required at least one running prototype of the vehicle for assessment. Depending upon the problem at hand, as many as six prototypes might have been built, including one for destructive firing testing of its armour protection.

4 **Factory Testing.** Once the prototype was ready, it underwent factory testing by the designers and engineers in concert with the 'Zakhacik' or customer representative (the Ministry of Defence representative to the plant). Once the major bugs had been ironed out and approval granted by the Scientific Committee, the vehicle was then sent for State Polygon (range) Testing at Kubinka.

5 **State Polygon Testing.** The military and members of the Ministry of Defence and Ministry of Defence Production authorities tested all major qualities of the new vehicle in a series of planned tests at the Kubinka Test Polygon. 'Findings' were made, which required the plant to repair or correct them as soon as possible. Once all corrections were made, permission was granted for troop testing.

6 Troop Testing. This usually required an establishment lot (*ustavlennaya partiya*) of vehicles to be built – usually a batch of 3, 5, 10 or 25 tanks, depending on the viability of the product and requirements for thorough testing. Vehicles might then be sent to various parts of the Soviet Union for testing – the north for winter conditions, the Southern Republics such as Kazakhstan for desert conditions, the Urals for mountainous conditions, etc. Once the vehicle passed its troop testing phase, the Ministry of Defence and Ministry of Defence Production would recommend it for acceptance and full production.

7 State Resolution. A joint resolution of the Central Committee of the Politburo of the Communist Party and the Council of Ministers of the USSR (many members holding positions in both) named the item (i.e. T-10, T-10A, T-10M, etc.) and announced it was accepted for service with the Soviet Army. Full production might then be ordered by the Ministry of Defence and Ministry of Defence Production (occasionally the project was tabled at this point due to extenuating circumstances, as for example the 100mm D-54TS armed T-62A tank), followed by the factory preparing to put the vehicle into full production. This might take place nearly immediately if it was only a modification of a vehicle in series production, or there might be as much as a year and a half delay while the plant remodelled and retooled to produce the new machine.

All this could take up to ten years of elapsed time from project to first production model rollout.

Once the vehicles were in service, there were set times and levels of repairs needed called TO-1, TO-2 and Capital Rebuilding. They were rebuilt under the capital rebuilding programme of the Soviet Army. Given the years listed and numbers, it is probable these tanks were all given major upgrades. The T-54s would be upgraded to T-54AM standards and the T-55s to any of the T-55M, T-55AM, T-55MV or T-55AMV standards. While some were to be retained for either reserve status, or for use with Soviet Naval Infantry in the case of the T-55AMV tanks, others would be sold abroad after the 1991 downfall of the Soviet Union.

Tanks were maintained as per four levels of maintenance that determined when they would be rebuilt.

The first level was daily technical inspection (EhTO) and covered routine tank operations on a daily basis. The checks included lubrication as defined in the maintenance manual, checking fluid levels for hydraulics, coolant and lubricants, track tension, air cleaner and in line filters, and any missing or damaged parts. This was crew level maintenance.

Technical Inspection 1 (TO-1) was carried out at set points of operation (either by mileage, time on the engine or usage period) and was more detailed, covering adjustments to the sights, equipment, brakes, track tension and condition of track shoes, hoses, lines, and most critical components. This was company level maintenance.

Technical Inspection 2 (TO-2) was more detailed than TO-1 and called for co ordinated work by higher level technical personnel with specialized equipment to adjust, align and service most key components of the tank. It could include bore-sighting the gun, aligning the IR equipment, checking radio and intercom operation, and replacing any worn out or service limited items. This was regimental or division level maintenance.

Capital rebuilding took place after the tank had covered 5,000 to 10,000 kilometres (based on tank model) or completed ten years of service. The tank would be shipped back to a specialized rebuilding plant where it would be stripped down and completely examined from the ground up. Worn out or obsolete components would be replaced, rebuilt engine and transmission installed, lines and hoses replaced, and any new upgraded components introduced at that time. These could include RMSh tracks in place of OMSh tracks, new road wheels, upgraded radio systems (R-123/R-173 for the older R-113, R-134 for the older R-112 in command tanks), new sights, thermal sleeves for the gun, smoke grenade launchers, demand fuel feed systems for the 200 litre auxiliary tanks, an NVST machine gun in place of the DShKM, and PKTs in place of the SGMs. Most tanks would have been limited to one capital rebuilding in their lifetime, but T-55s seem to have had two – especially if they were going to be sold to a foreign client.

While in service, there were four categories of serviceability for the tanks:

- **Category 1:** vehicle is new, fully combat capable, all systems are fully operational, all spare parts and tools are in place, and the vehicle is ready to go.
- **Category 2:** vehicle is used, mostly combat capable, needs some minor repairs to some systems, may be missing some spare parts and tools, but could stand in a combat formation.
- **Category 3:** vehicle is in need of major repairs; some combat systems are inoperable or no longer present in the vehicle, it is missing most

of its spare parts and tools, and would not be sufficiently capable of conducting combat.

- **Category 4:** vehicle is nearly inoperable, suffers from major failures of key systems (engine, driveline, gun, operating mechanisms) and needs capital repair or rebuilding.

There is a Category 5, which signifies the vehicle has been written off (peacetime) or is a 'non-returning combat loss' (wartime). In some cases, vehicles in this condition were stripped of most running gear, supporting systems, and electronics, and then dug in as pillboxes or firing points in fortified regions such as along the mainland Chinese border or on Soviet Sakhalin Island in the Pacific Ocean.

APPENDIX EIGHT
GLOSSARY

ATGM:	Anti-Tank Guided Missile
BTS:	Bronyevoy Tyagach Sredny or Sredny Tankovy Tyagach – Medium Tank Tractor
ChKZ:	Chelyabinsky Kirovsky Zavod (ChTZ from 15.05.58)
ChTZ:	Chelyabinsky Traktorny Zavod imeni V.I. Lenina (ChKZ before 15.05.58)
GABTU:	Gosudarstvennoye Avtomotivnoye Bronetankirovannoye Upravleniye – Main Automotive and Armoured Vehicle Directorate
GBTU:	Gosudarstvennoye Bronetankirovannoye Upravleniye – Main Armoured Vehicle Directorate
HEAT:	High Explosive Anti-tank
IMR:	Inzhenirnaya Mashina Razgrazhdeniya – Engineer Obstacle Clearing Vehicle
LVZ:	Leningrad Voroshilov Plant (Plant No. 174 in Omsk)
KB:	Konstruktorskoye Byuro – Design Bureau
KBTM:	Konstruktorskoye Byuro Transportivnoy Mashinoy – Design Bureau for Transport Vehicles (Omsk)
MBT:	Main Battle Tank
MO:	Ministerstvo Oboroni – Soviet (Russian) Ministry of Defence (MoD)
MTO:	Motorno-Transmissionaya Otdel' – Motor Transmission Compartment

MTrM:	Ministerstvo Trasportivnoy Mashinikh Promishlennosti – Ministry of Transport Machinery Construction
NKVD:	Narodny Kommisariat Vnutrenikh Del – Peoples' Commissariat for Internal Affairs
NST:	Novy Sredny Tank – New Medium Tank
OPVT:	Oborudovaniye Podvodnoy Vozhdeniya Tanki – Underwater Tank Driving Equipment
PAZ:	Protivoatomnoi Zashiti – Anti-nuclear Protection
PPO:	Protivo-Pozharnoye Oborudovaniye – Fire Suppression Equipment
RPG:	Rocket-Propelled Grenade (launcher)
SM SSSR:	Sovet Ministerov SSSR – Council of Ministers of the USSR
TDA:	Termal'naya Dymovaya Apparata – Thermal Smoke Generation Apparatus
TPU:	Tankovoe Peregovornoe Ustroistva – Tank Verbal Communications System
TsK KPSU:	Tsentral'ny Komitet Kommunicheskoy Partii Sovetskogo Soyuza – Central Committee of the Communist Party of the Soviet Union
TsNII-6:	Central Scientific Research Institutes for Flame Weapons, Moscow
TsNII-48:	Central Scientific Research Institute for Armour, Leningrad
TsNII-173:	Central Scientific Research Institute for Artillery Stabilizers, Moscow
UVZ:	Ural'ny Vagonstroitel'sviy Zavod – Urals Railway Wagon Construction Factory
VNII-100:	Vsesoyuzny Nauchno-Issledovatelsky Institut (later VNII Transmash)
Zavod No. 9:	Artillery Plant No. 9, Perm (F. F. Petrov Bureau)
Zavod No. 75:	Kharkov Tank Plant (formerly Kharkov Diesel Engine Construction Plant)
Zavod No. 174:	Omsk Tank Plant (formerly in Leningrad)
Zavod No. 183:	Urals Railway Wagon Construction Plant, Nizhny Tagil (formerly Kharkov Steam Locomotive Construction Plant in Kharkov, today Kharkiv)
Zavod No. 393:	Optical Plant, Krasnogorsk (the Zenit Plant)

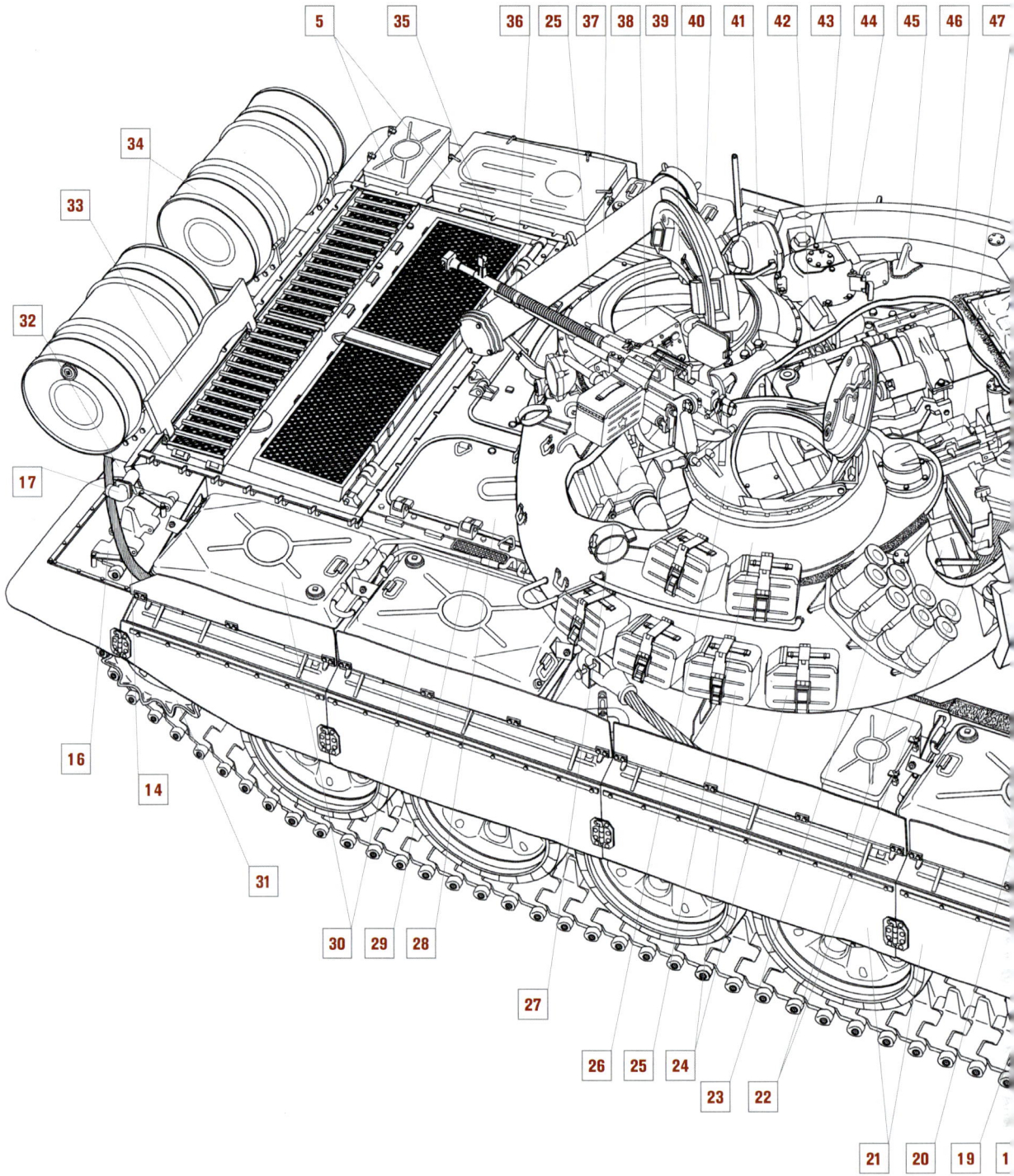

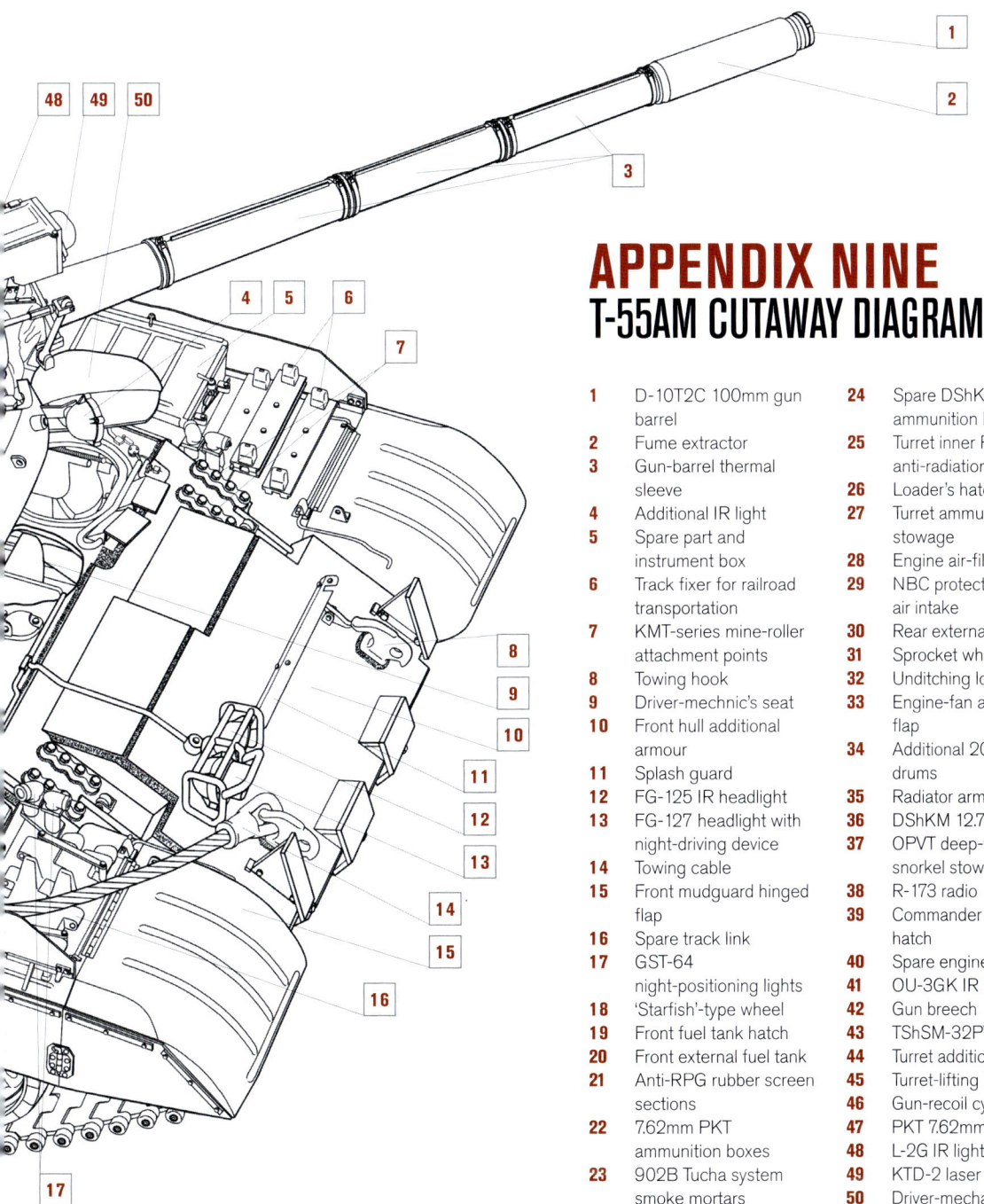

APPENDIX NINE
T-55AM CUTAWAY DIAGRAM

1	D-10T2C 100mm gun barrel	**24**	Spare DShKM 12.7mm ammunition boxes
2	Fume extractor	**25**	Turret inner POV-50 anti-radiation layer
3	Gun-barrel thermal sleeve	**26**	Loader's hatch
4	Additional IR light	**27**	Turret ammunition stowage
5	Spare part and instrument box	**28**	Engine air-filter hatch
6	Track fixer for railroad transportation	**29**	NBC protection system air intake
7	KMT-series mine-roller attachment points	**30**	Rear external fuel tanks
8	Towing hook	**31**	Sprocket wheel
9	Driver-mechnic's seat	**32**	Unditching log
10	Front hull additional armour	**33**	Engine-fan armoured flap
11	Splash guard	**34**	Additional 200-litre fuel drums
12	FG-125 IR headlight	**35**	Radiator armoured cover
13	FG-127 headlight with night-driving device	**36**	DShKM 12.7mm MG
14	Towing cable	**37**	OPVT deep-wading snorkel stowage
15	Front mudguard hinged flap	**38**	R-173 radio
16	Spare track link	**39**	Commander cupola hatch
17	GST-64 night-positioning lights	**40**	Spare engine oil tank
18	'Starfish'-type wheel	**41**	OU-3GK IR light
19	Front fuel tank hatch	**42**	Gun breech
20	Front external fuel tank	**43**	TShSM-32PV gun sight
21	Anti-RPG rubber screen sections	**44**	Turret additional armour
22	7.62mm PKT ammunition boxes	**45**	Turret-lifting hook
23	902B Tucha system smoke mortars	**46**	Gun-recoil cylinders
		47	PKT 7.62mm coaxial MG
		48	L-2G IR light
		49	KTD-2 laser rangefinder
		50	Driver-mechanic's hatch

APPENDIX TEN
SOVIET/RUSSIAN COMMUNICATIONS SYSTEMS AND DEVELOPMENT

Unlike previous Soviet tanks (many of which also lasted into the new Russian era), the T-55 underwent a number of changes in its communications equipment and suite over both the course of production and its lifespan. These paralleled developments in their overall communications systems in general and tactical communications in particular.

During the 1930s and into World War II the Soviet military used low-power, low-level high frequency (HF) amplitude modulated (AM) radio sets, usually operating between 2 and 6 megahertz (MHz). They were vulnerable to weather conditions, burned-out tubes, vibration, and other maladies of the day that could limit their effectiveness, and even under the best of conditions range with voice communications was less than 15–20 kilometres, and when used with a manual Morse code key only about 40 kilometres.

Two things occurred during World War II that gave the Soviets a new perspective on tactical communications. The Germans fielded command vehicles with specially fitted radio sets to allow commanders to co-ordinate tank, mechanized infantry and artillery actions or to communicate directly with tactical support aircraft like dive bombers or anti-tank hunters. However, like all Soviet radio sets these were all HF AM radio sets.

Through Lend-Lease the Soviet Union received a large number of American armoured vehicles, all of which were primarily equipped with the SCR-508/510/608/610 series radio sets. These were all very high frequency (VHF) sets working on frequency modulation (FM) that permitted much

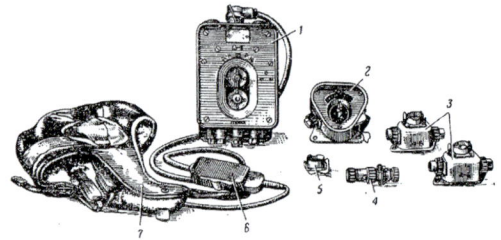

ABOVE LEFT The R-113 VHF FM transceiver with a frequency range of 20–22.5 MHz. This provided communications of up to 15–20 kilometres.
ABOVE RIGHT The 'shlemofon' headset/helmet and the R-120 intercom communications control boxes for the crew. 1 is the commander's control with intercom/radio switch and 2 is the box for the other three crew members.
LEFT The improved R-123 VHF FM transceiver with a frequency range of 20–51.5 MHz, which permitted interaction with other arms of service. The range was 20–25 kilometres.

better and clearer communications over 20–25 kilometres. The sets also had frequency overlap, so a unit with armour radios could communicate with mechanized infantry or artillery at the ends of the frequency band, which was a much better working arrangement.

After the war the Soviet Union began to do major research on VHF systems, and by the 1950s it began to deploy its first series of VHF FM radios and the first command and control radio stations based on those sets. The first major innovation was the TPU-47 (Tankovoe Peregovornoe Ustroistva), a tank intercom system introduced in 1947 that permitted all of the crewmembers to communicate directly with each other within the tank. However, for the initial period of introduction, the tanks retained the 10-RT-26 (HF AM) radio sets from the end of the war.

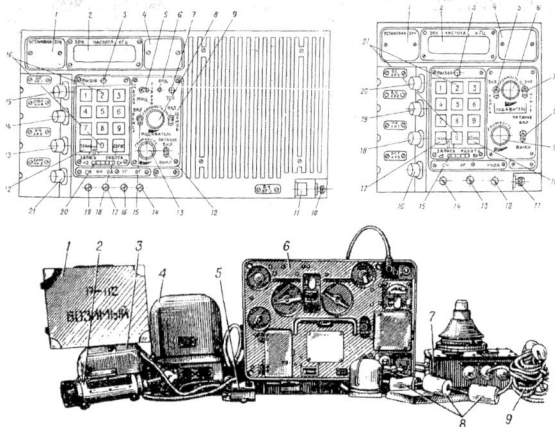

The first Soviet FM set specifically designed for armour, which went straight into the new T-55 tank in 1958, was the R-113 set. While it was limited in frequency range (20–22 MHz), it was coupled to the improved R-120 intercom system and was a great step forward in tank unit communications. Battalion level commanders received tanks with two of these sets, and regimental commanders received tanks that were also fitted with the improved R-112 HF AM set (frequency range 1.5–4.2 MHz) and a 10-metre antenna for use while stopped. This gave them reliable communications via the R-113 and up to 100 kilometres with Morse on the R-112.

However, the limited frequency ranges resulted in what radio operators call being 'stepped on', with too many units using the same narrow frequency bands. In the late 1960s, new equipment was developed and issued, starting with the R-123 radio set and R-124 intercom system. The R-123 was a much better set with up to four frequency presets and increased output, but most welcome was its expanded frequency range of 20–51.5 MHz, which both permitted wider use and also easy co-ordination with motorized rifle and artillery units and their dedicated radio sets (the artillery used the R-108 from 28–36.5 MHz and the motorized rifles the R-105 (36–46.1 MHz)).

Initially battalion commanders had two R-123 sets, but with the presets in the R-123 they soon received an HF set instead. While at first they used the R-112 as before, later it was upgraded to the newer R-130 9 (frequency

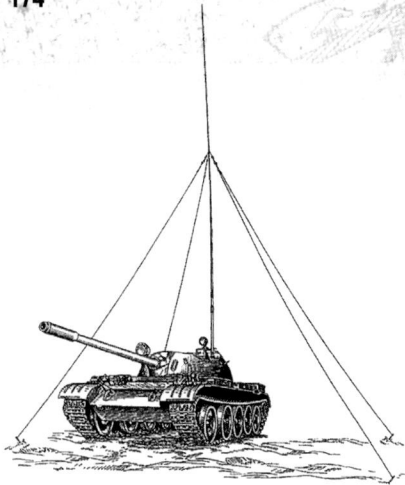

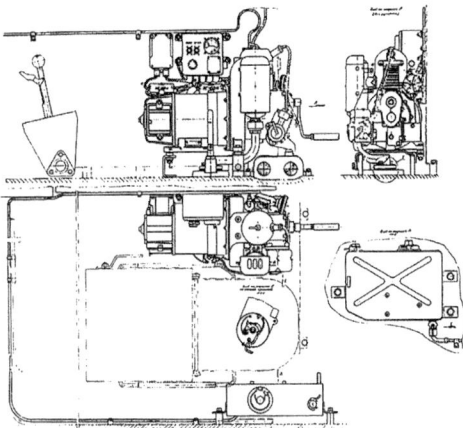

TOP The manual drawing of the 11-metre antenna for fixed site use when erected on command tanks.

ABOVE The auxiliary generator for use at fixed sites by command tanks. It replaced the bow machine gun and its ammunition as well as five rounds in the 'stellazh' rack.

range 1.5–10.99 MHz). The R-130 was also optimized for what are referred to as single sideband 'skywave' communications, where the signal is bounced off the ionosphere, so now a battalion commander could communicate up to 350 kilometres with the right antenna and weather conditions.

As the T-55s came in for midlife rebuilding, they generally all received the aforementioned communications upgrades, so by the 1970s most of the tanks had the R-123/R-124 and R-130 configurations.

In the 1980s the Soviet Union began to adopt its first solid state radio sets, and of course that meant new radios for the tactical level. The new tactical set was the R-173, which was even more advanced, with a frequency range of 30–79.90 MHz (similar to NATO and US sets). It could store up to ten preset frequencies and also could be used for both analogue and digital communications systems. It was paired with the improved R-174 intercom system. The HF command sets were upgraded to the R-134 series radios (frequency range 1.5–29.99 MHz). As older T-55 tanks were upgraded to M status with new engines, fire controls, ATGM capability and other improvements, they also received these new radio sets.

While only a handful of T-55s remain in service with the Russian military today, many of the tanks are still in service with foreign clients, hence new and modern communications suites are also offered, most involving the use of the new R-168 family of digital radio sets. These have a broad range of frequencies depending on model, but the main VHF versions now cover 30–108 MHz.

With full upgrades such as reactive armour, laser range finders, the 1K13 fire control system, a new engine, tracks, survival equipment and electronics, the Soviet-era T-55 remains today a very effective second tier combat vehicle.

Note that most Soviet tankers used the 'shlemofon', which was a padded helmet with built-in headsets and a strap-on throat microphone; a chest switch was used for transmitting on the selected radio set. However, the throat microphone needed to be relatively tight to work properly, and if not adjusted correctly the user tended to sound somewhat like Donald Duck when speaking.

APPENDIX ELEVEN
SOVIET BALLISTIC SETS AND TABLES

While politically the Soviet Union witnessed some internal extremes and dynamic movements, when it came to engineering and science, the Soviet Union and its designers were very methodical, thorough, and practical. One such methodology was the determination of a set of ballistic standards and their application to all weapons of a given calibre and gun barrel specification.

Soviet weapon designers from the outset understood that all guns using similar ammunition and barrel length would have nearly identical ballistic tables and results. It made no difference if it was a machine gun, automatic cannon, mortar, howitzer or gun – all weapons of that calibre with that length of barrel would fire with near identical performance. Also irrelevant was its platform – field gun, tank, railway, or ship. So tables were created based on the types of ammunition used and were therefore standardized by all arms plants to permit easier development of sights, equipment, accessories and, most of all, ammunition.

The sets were given a specific number, and when developing sights or other accessories the relevant factory would have a set standard to use at once. For example, a 7.62mm machine gun, no matter whether it was a DT, SGM, SGMT, or PKT type, would use the same set of ballistics – Set 11. Likewise, the 14.5mm KPV and KPVT would use Set 14.

The 76.2mm guns on the wartime tanks with a 41.5-calibre long barrel – either the F-34 or the ZiS-5 – used Set 7. The early T-34-85 tanks used Set 15, but with more powerful ammunition it was upgraded to Set 16.

The T-54 and T-55 used three different sets of ballistic tables. The very early models used Set 20, but the production versions used Set 22. Later, when HEAT ammunition and then sabot (APDS) rounds were introduced, they used Set 32.

The TSh2B-32P direct fire telescopic sight used in the T-55 series tanks.

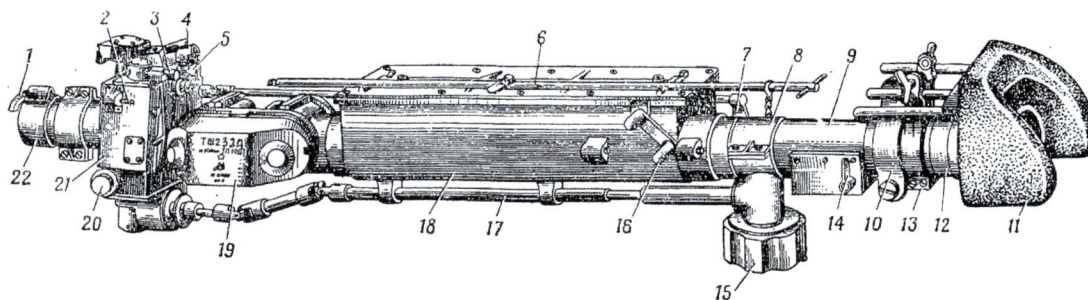

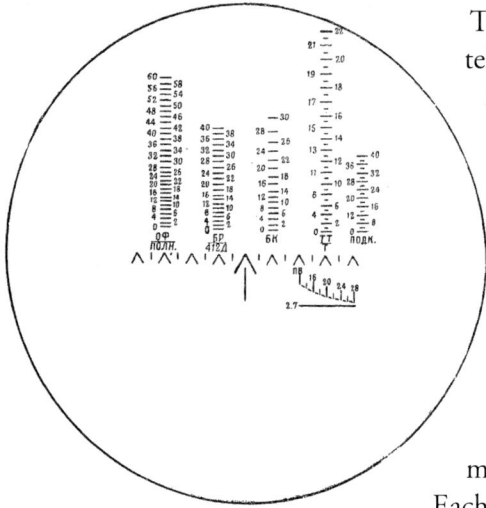

The recticule used by the T2Sh-32P telescopic sight. The difference between ballistic table 22 and ballistic table 32 is the inclusion of the BK adjustment scale (third one from the left) and the sub-calibre table (far right), as well as the OF high-explosive and BP armour-piercing scales. The TT scale is for the 7.62mm machine gun.

These sets are part of the designator for the sight, and that tells the crew and the support staff what reticule is installed in the telescopic or direct fire sight. For example, the T-34-85 used either a TSh-15 or TSh-16 sight based on the production date and type of ammunition. A T-10 used the TSh2-27, with the number indicating the table for the post-war 122mm gun, whereas the T-10M used a T2S-29-14 day sight and a TPS-1-29-14 night sight; Set 29 was for the 122mm M-62 gun with improved ballistics and Set 14 indicated the co-axial 14.5mm KPVT heavy machine gun.

The T-54 started out with the TSh-20 sight, later moving on to the T2S-22 and finally the T2S-32 series. Each number indicated an improved set of ballistics with better ammunition types. The T-55 used the TSh-2B-22; then the TSh-32; next the TShSM-32; and last the TShSM-32PV with single-axis stabilized view (vertical plane).

The installed bespoke reticules provided the deviation distance and lead percentage at range for each type of ammunition to cover the ballistic drop of the projectile and compensate for its velocity over distance. A different number and shift would be needed for armour piercing (around 900 metres/second) and high explosive (around 730 metres/second). Likewise, the use of HEAT rounds at lower velocities and APDS and later APFSDS rounds with much higher velocities had to be provided for as well.

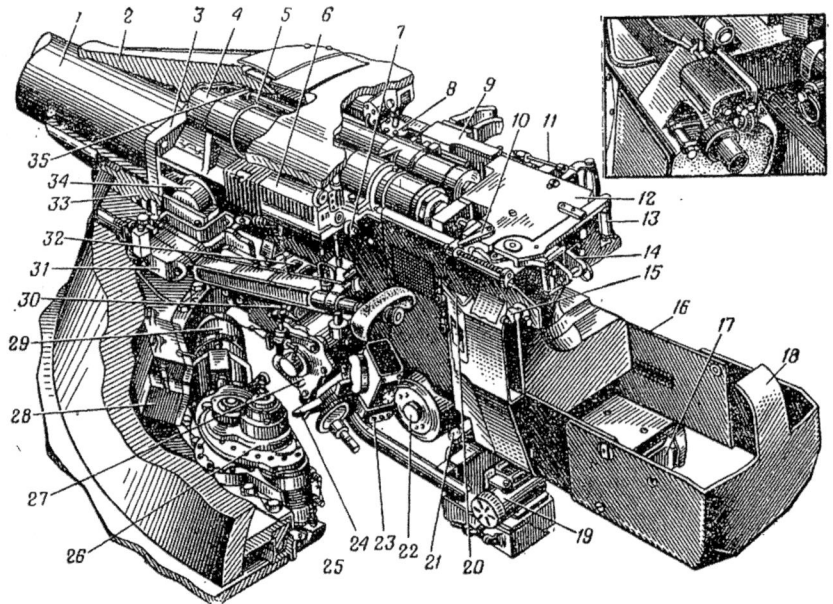

A schematic of the gunner's position in a T-55 Model 1958, showing the arrangement of the sight and gunner's controls. 'Cadillac' fire controls were not introduced until much later in the tank's life, when it received the 'M' series upgrades.

APPENDIX TWELVE
OPVT UNDERWATER TANK DRIVING EQUIPMENT

Since tanks obviously do not float as designed, tank designers in several countries for a number of years worked on methods to permit armoured vehicles to cross water obstacles of relatively narrow span and shallow depth. The Wehrmacht developed one design for their Pzkpfw III tanks for the planned invasion of England called Tauschpanzer (Diving Tank), which sealed the tank and provided an air intake via a floating flexible snorkel. While the Wehrmacht used it to cross some rivers with moderate success, it was never a standardized feature.

The Soviet Union had in the meantime also expended considerable effort since the 1930s in the development of water crossing capability for armoured vehicles. In the western states of the Soviet Union, and in Western Europe, there are many small streams and tributaries. These water obstacles are encountered roughly every 15–20 kilometres, with most being less than five metres deep. The designers at UVZ in the post-war era thereby also worked on a method to permit their tanks to cross such obstacles without either swimming equipment (bulky and awkward) or assault bridging (difficult under fire). Such a lightweight 'temporary' solution was introduced at UVZ on the final production versions of the T-54B tank, and then immediately adapted for use on the later T-55 as it entered series production.

FAR LEFT A manual schematic of a T-55 Model 1958 as rigged for underwater driving with the two-section snorkel erected.

BELOW The original Soviet-designed cover for the radiator air intake and exhaust at the rear of the hull. The hatch was kept open until the tank was to enter the water to prevent overheating. Early models used brackets welded to the side of the engine deck to attach it; later models had a fixed raised frame above the engine deck.

BOTTOM The pressure-operated flapper mechanism for the engine exhaust to prevent water backflow from killing the engine under water.

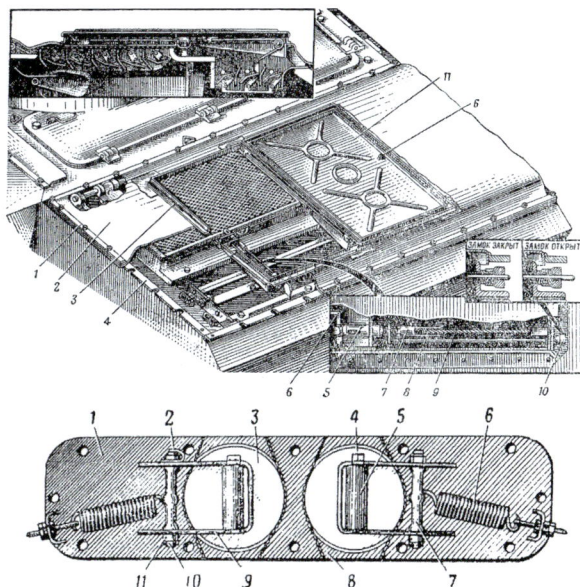

The equipment – Oborudovaniye dlya Podvodnogo Vozhdenniya Tanka (OPVT) or equipment for underwater driving of tanks – began to be issued in early 1958. Its purpose was to permit the tank to autonomously cross a water obstacle of up to 700 metres wide with a depth of 5 metres or less and also permit the tank to emerge from the water combat-ready with a safe crew. It provided air to the crew and engine, prevented water from flooding and stalling the engine while underwater, ensured the tank could move underwater in a given direction, and provided for the tank to be completely mobile when it left the water.

To this end, OPVT systems consisted of a number of components:

- A two-section snorkel tube roughly 4 metres long when assembled;
- An exhaust flapper valve providing one-way flow of the exhaust;
- Covers for the radiator air intake;
- Covers for the gun muzzle, gunner's sight aperture, machine gun port, and antenna feed and base;

RIGHT The bilge pump for T-55s that was located in the front left corner of the engine compartment. The pump had an irreversible valve to prevent water ingress and exited under the right rear edge of the turret (not visible until the turret was removed).

BELOW LEFT The GKN-48 gyrocompass in front of the driver-mechanic to keep him on course when under water.

BELOW RIGHT The final stowage position for the two-section snorkel under the twin 200-litre auxiliary fuel tanks. This one is fitted with a guard to prevent damage from the rear.

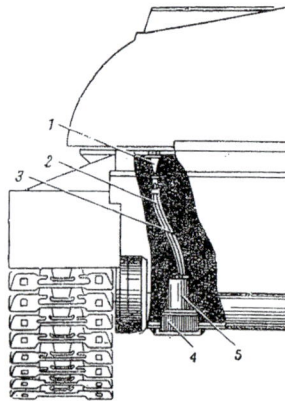

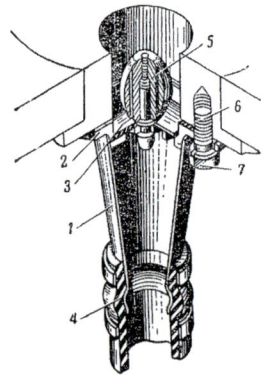

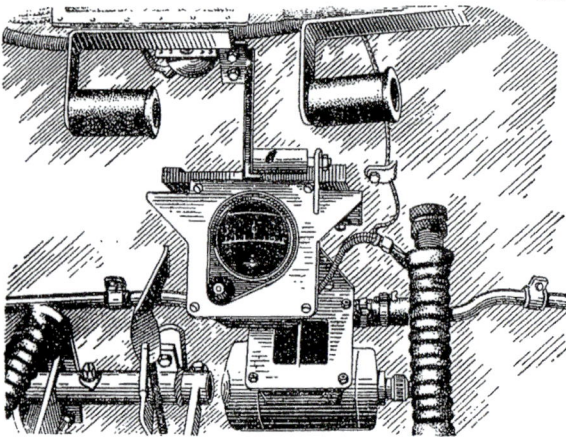

TOP A T-55 Model 1958 at the Kubinka Museum with the two-section snorkel in place, mounted in the stead of the gunner's MK-4 vision device.

LEFT The three-section snorkel erected; note the depth marks on the snorkel for shore observers to track the depth of the water.

ABOVE A late model T-55 that has been retrofitted with the 1969 changes to include external ammunition racks for the 12.7mm machine gun and the four-section snorkel stowed on the front right side of the turret. The tank was converted from an OT-55 flamethrower tank.

- Cover for the air feed to the transfer case (guitara);
- Sealing for the turret, ventilator, ZIP bins, and hatches;
- A bilge pump at the rear of the hull fitted with a one-way valve to bail out water collecting on the floor of the engine compartment (apparently introduced on the T-55);
- Life jackets and rebreathers for crew escape if necessary;
- A GPK-48 gyrocompass for underwater navigation.

The intent was to carry all of this equipment on the tank, but it is not obvious if that was completely possible. The major problem item was the two-section snorkel, which even in its collapsed state was about 1.75 metres long and 15cm in diameter. It was eventually installed in brackets on top of the 200-litre auxiliary fuel tanks on production tanks and later mounted under them in conversions of T-54 Model 1949, Model 1951 and T-54A tanks and the early T-55 tanks.

To prepare the tank for crossing, all of the seals were checked first and drain plugs installed in the hull floor of the tank. The snorkel was removed, to be bolted together with seals between sections and base, the loader's MK-4 viewing device was removed from its mount, and the assembled snorkel was attached in its place with bolts. Steps were mounted to the snorkel for the use of rescue personnel to climb up and contact the crew if the tank stalled. The covers were attached to their specific items with clamps and the flapper valve installed to the exhaust outlet.

The entire engine deck area was covered by a rubber-impregnated canvas cover that was bolted down to the edges of a frame. It had a fixed metal frame in the middle with a folding and sealing hatch cover to permit airflow on land without removing the cover. The engine radiator air intake had five moveable internal louvres that could be adjusted to cut off outside airflow, but the cover prevented water ingress.

Once the tank was prepared, a seal around the inside of the turret race was inflated to prevent water entry into the tank. Some leakage was expected and charts told the crew what was acceptable; once the tank began crossing the bilge pump would be turned on to evacuate water that did seep into the tank, but it was only after the tank exited the water that it could fully clear the engine compartment.

The actual crossing usually required prepared banks on both sides of the obstacle or at least shallow approaches to the river or creek. The tank would move into the water in first gear at an engine speed of 1500rpm to make the crossing. The driver-mechanic would use the GPK-48 gyrocompass to keep the tank heading in the right direction. Once across, the tank could fire on targets immediately if needed, but this would destroy the muzzle and machine gun covers. The tank would start to overheat if the hatch over the engine deck was not opened soon after crossing, and the tanks could obviously not sit at idle for a long time with no air circulation.

For night crossings, a cable would be dropped down the snorkel and a red light similar to the marker and tail lights fitted to the top, so the commander could follow the progress of his tanks across the water.

As might be expected, there were accidents during training and exercises, and usually tow cables would be run to the tanks to ensure that if the tanks stalled they could be hauled out of the water. Often (as in East Germany), the places where training took place were purpose-built concrete basin-like structures to make it easy to enter, cross and exit.

BELOW LEFT A Czech T-55A fording a water obstacle with the combat snorkel erected. This one appears to have the three-section combat snorkel.

BELOW Another Czech T-55A but fitted with the larger training snorkel. This attached to the loader's hatch and had ladder rungs inside and outside for the crew to escape if necessary.

Several changes in design took place over the years. One was the introduction of a larger training snorkel that bolted to the commander's cupola and allowed the crew easy exit if the tank stalled. Another was an antenna feed to the top of the snorkel for an antenna allowing communications to the tank via radio. Both were developed for crew safety and also to reduce the number of accidents. If the driver-mechanic did not switch on the GPK-48 to give him a bearing, the worst problem was that the tank would turn 90° toward downstream and go with the flow rather than across it.

Around 1965, the Soviet Army moved to a smaller, more compact snorkel arrangement using a four-section snorkel that closed down to just over one metre in length. This was now moved to a new stowage location on the sides or rear of the tank's turret, as the other stowage positions for the two-section snorkel were vulnerable to damage.

The Soviet Union experimented with a wading device in lieu of the OPVT equipment, using a raised skirt over the engine deck like the Allied World War II 'Duplex Drive' tanks to permit the tank to ford to about two metres. It is fitted with an exhaust deflector tube rather than a flapper device. In the end the designers kept with the OPVT system.

BIBLIOGRAPHY

BOOKS – RUSSIAN LANGUAGE

Babazhanyan, A. Kh., *Tanki I Tankovye Voyska* (Voyennoye Izdatel'stvo, 1980)

Baranov, I. N. (general editor), *Glavny Konstruktor V. N. Venediktov: Zhizn' Otdannaya Tankam* (DiAl, Nizhny Tagil, 2009)

Baryatinskiy, Mikhail, *1945–2008: Sovetskye Tanki v Boyu* (Yauza/Ehksmo, 2008)

Baryatinskiy, Mikhail, *Tanki v Chechnye – Sovetskaya Bronetankovaya Tekhika v 'Goryachikh Tochkakh' SSSR I SNG 1989–1998 gg.* (Zhelezhnodoroznoye Delo, Moscow, 1999)

Baryatinskiy, Mikhail, *Tanki XX Vek – Unikal'naya Entsiklopediya* (Yauza/ Ehksmo, 2010)

Baushev, I., ed., *Sozdateli Oruzhiya I Voyennoy Tekhniki Sukhoputnykh Voysk Rossii* (Pashkov Dom, Moscow, 2008)

Bryukhov, Vasily P., *Bronetankovye Voyska* (Golos Press, Moscow, 2006)

Bryzgov, V., and Yermolina, O., *Bronetankovaya Tekhnika – Fotoal'bom* (Gonchar, Moscow, 1994)

Chernyshev, Vladimir L., ed., *Tanki I Lyudi: Dnevnik Glavnogo Konstruktora Aleksandra Aleksandrovicha Morozova* (internet version published on http:// www.btvt.narod.ru, 2006/2007) (translated by author)

Drogovoz, Igor G., *Tankovy Mech Strany Sovetov* (Kharvest, Minsk, 2001)

Fes'kov, V. I., Kalashnikov, K. A., and Golikov, V. I., *Sovetskaya Armya v Gody 'Kholodnoy Voyny' (1945–1991)* (Tomsk State University, Tomsk, 2004)

Ionin, S. N., *Bronetankovye Voyska SSSR-Rossii* (Veche, Moscow, 2006)

Karpenko, A. V., *Obozrenye Otechestvennoy Bronetankovoy Tekhniki (1905–1995 gg.)* (Nevsky Bastion, St. Petersburg, 1996)

Karyakin, L. A., and Moiseyev, V. I., *Voyennye Tekhniki I Vooruzhenye Kitaya – Vyp. 1: Tanki* (Krasny Oktyabr, Saransk, 2002)

Kholyavskiy, G. L., *Entsiklopediya Bronyetekhniki – Gusenichnye Boyevye Mashiny* (Kharvest, Minsk, 2001)

Lavrenov, S. Ya., *Sovetsky Soyuz v Lokal'nykh Voynakh I Konfliktakh* (Astrel', Moscow, 2003)

Minayev, A. V. (general editor), *Sovetskaya Voyennaya Moshch: Ot Stalina do Gorbacheva* (Voyenny Parad, 1999)

Ministry of Defence Publications, *Rukovodstvo po Eksplotatsii Tanka T-44* (Moscow, 1946)

Ministry of Defence Publications, *Rukovodstvo po Material'noy Chasti I Ekspluatsii Tanka T-55* (Moscow, 1969)

Ministry of Defence Publications, *Rukovodstvo po Material'noy Chasti I Ekspluatsii Tanka T-62* (Moscow, 1968)

Ministry of Defence Publications, *Tank T-55AM: Dopolneniye k Tekhicheskomy Opisanyu I Instruktsii po Eksplatatsii Tanka T-55* (Voyenizdat, Moscow, 1983)

Moskovsky, A. G. (general editor), *75 Let Upravleniyu Nachal'nika Vooruzheniya* (Voyenny Parad, Moscow, 2004)

Pavlov, M., Pavlov, I., and Zheltov, I., Polonskiy, V. A. (chairman of the editorial group), *Glavnoye Avtobronetankovoye Upravenye: Lyudi, Sobytiya, Fakty v Dokumentakh 1946–1953 gg.*, Book V (Ministry of Defence of the Russian Federation, Moscow, 2007)

Popov, N. S., Petrov, V. I., Popov, A. N., and Ashik, M. V., *Bez Tayn I Sekretov* (Prana, St. Petersburg, 1995)

Popov. N. S., Yefremov, A. S., and Ashik, M. V., *Tank, Brosivshiy Vyzov Vremeni* (Kaskad Poligrafiya, St. Petersburg, 2001)

Reznik, Yakov, *Sotvorenie Broni* (Voyennoye Izdatel'stvo, Moscow, 1983)

Rogoza, S. L., and Achkasov, N. B., *Zasekrechennye Voyny 1950–2000 gg.* (AST, St. Petersburg, 2004)

Safonov, B. S., and Murakhovsky, V. I., *Osnovnye Boyevye Tanki* (Arsenal-Press, Moscow, 1993)

Shirokorad, A. B., *Entsiklopediya Otechestvennoy Artillerii* (Kharvest, Minsk, 2000)

Shumulin, S. Eh., *T-54/55 Sovestky Osnovnoy Tank Chast' 1*; Voyennno-Tekhnicheskaya Serya No. 102 (ATF, Kharkov, 1998)

Shumulin, S. Eh., *T-54/55 Sovestky Osnovnoy Tank Chast' 2,* Voyennno-Tekhnicheskaya Serya No. 103 (ATF, Kharkov, 1998)

Shumulin, S. Eh., Okolelov, N., and Chechin, A., *Sredny Tank T-55,* Bronekollektsya No. 4 (79) (Modellist Konstruktor, Moscow, 2008)

Solyankin, A. G., *Bronetankovaya Tekhnika Sovetskoy Armii – Al'bom* (Ministry of Defence Publishing, Moscow, 1983)

Solyankin, A. G., Pavlov, M. V., Pavlov, I. V., and Zheltov, I. G., *Otechestvennye Bronirovannye Mashiny XX Vek: Tom 2 – Otechestvennye Bronirovannye Mashiny 1941–1945* (Exprint, Moscow, 2005)

Solyankin, A. G., Zheltov, I. G., and Kudryashov, K. N., *Otechestvennye Bronirovannye Mashiny XX Vek: Tom 3 – Otechestvennye Bronirovannye Mashiny 1945–1965* (Tseykhgauz, Moscow, 2010)

Svirin, Mikhail, *Armada Vertikal' No. 4: Artilleriyskoye Vooruzhenye Sovetskikh Tankov 1940–1945* (Exprint, 1999)

Svirin, Mikhail, *Stal'noy Kulak Stalina: Istorya Sovetskogo Tanka 1943–1955* (Yauza/Eksmo, 2006)

Svirin, Mikhail, *Tankovaya Moshch' SSSR : Pervaya Polnaya Ehntsiklopediya* (Yauza/Eksmo, 2009)

Ust'yantsev, S., and Kolmakov, D., *Boyevye Mashiny Uralvagonzavoda: Tanki T-54/T55*, Part 3 (Dom 'Media-Print', Nizhny Tagil, 2006) (translated by author)

Ust'yantsev, S., and Kolmakov, D., *Boyevye Mashiny Uralvagonzavoda: Tanki 60-ikh*, Part 4 (Dom 'Media-Print', Nizhny Tagil, 2007) (translated by author)

Vasilyeva, L., and Zheltov, I., *Nikolay Kucherenko: Pyat'desyat Let v Bitve za Tanki SSSR* (Atlantida – XXI Vek/Moskovskye Uchebniki, 2009) (translated by author)

Veretrennikov, A., Rasskazov, I., Sidorov, K., and Reshetilo, Y., *Kharkovskoye Konstruktorskoye Byuro po Mashinostroyenyu imeni A. A. Morozova* (IRIS Press, Kharkov, 1998)

Veretrennikov, A., Rasskazov, I., Sidorov, K., and Reshetilo, Y., *Kharkovskoye Konstruktorskoye Byuro po Mashinostroyenyu imeni A. A. Morozova* (IRIS Press, Kharkov, 2007)

Zayets, A. R. and Bronya, R., *Evolutsiya boyevikh I spetsial'nykh bronirovannykh mashin v Sovetsvogo Soyuza I Rossii posle Vtoroy Mirovoy Voyny – Kratky Ocherk* (Gumanitarny Universitet, 2002)

BOOKS – ENGLISH LANGUAGE

Hull, Andrew, Markov, David, and Zaloga, Steven, *Soviet/Russian Armor and Artillery Design Practices: 1945 to the Present* (Darlington Publications, Darlington, Maryland, 1999)

Kahalani, Avigdor, *The Heights of Courage: A Tank Leader's War on the Golan* (Greenwood Press, Westport, CT, 1984)

Magnewski, Janusz, *Combat Vehicles of the People's Polish Armed Forces 1943–1983* (FBIS Translation, October 1989)

Scott, Harriet F., and Scott, William F., *The Armed Forces of the USSR* (Westview Press, Boulder, CO, 1979)

PERIODICALS – RUSSIAN LANGUAGE

Bastion (St. Petersburg):

Karpenko, A. P., *No. 8/2000 – Otechestvennye Samokhodnye I Zenitnye Arterilliyskye Ustanovki Pt 1*

Karpenko, A. P., *No. 3/2001 –Otechestvennye Samokhodnye I Zenitnye Arterilliyskye Ustanovki Pt 2*

Bronekollektiysa (Moscow):

Baryatinskiy, M., *No. 2/2004 – Sredny Tank T-62*

Frontovaya Illyustratsya (Moscow)

Krasnaya Zvezda (Moscow)

Modelist-Konstruktor (Moscow)

Tankomaster (Moscow):

Karpenko, A. P., *No. 4/2001 – Tyazhelye Samokhodnye Artilleriyskye Ustanovky*

Karpenko, A. P., *No. 1/2002 – Srednye Samokhodnye Artillersiyskye Ustanovky*

Gold Collection, BMP-1 (1964–2000) – 2001

M-Khobbi (Moscow)

Tekhnika I Oruzhiye (Moscow)

Shirokorad, A., *No. 6/1996 – Samokhodnye Artilleriyskiye Ustanovky*

Tekhnika I Vooruzhenye (pre-1991 Soviet issues)

Tekhnika I Vooruzhenye: Vchera, Segondya, Zaftra (Moscow):

continuing series by L. N. Kartsev from January to November 2008: *Vospominaniya Glavnogo Konstruktora Tankov*

continuing series by L. N. Kartsev with Petr Kirichenko from October 2005 to January 2006 (Translated via DNI Open Source Center): *The Creators of Domestic Armored Vehicles*

continuing series by M. V. Pavlov and I. V. Pavlov from January 2009 to at least April 2014:

Otechestvennye Bronirovannye Mashiny 1945–1965 gg.

PERIODICALS – ENGLISH LANGUAGE

Armor (US Army)

AFV Profile (London):

Norman, Major Michael, *No. 23 – Soviet Mediums T44, T54, T55 & T62*

International Defence Review

Jane's Defence Review

MANUFACTURER'S BROCHURES AND DATASHEETS

Federal State Unitary Enterprise Design Bureau of Transport Machine
    Building (OKBTM Omsk):
    Modernizirovanny Tank T-55 (T-55M5) (Russian language)
    Shestikatkovy Tank T-55 (Maketny Obrazets) (T-55M6) (Russian language)
    *BTR-T Heavy Armoured Personnel Carrier (BTR-T) on the Base of the T-55
    tank* (English language)

ONLINE SOURCES

'Gur Khan Attacks' – http://gurkhan.blogspot.com/
'Soldat.ru' – http://www.soldat.ru/
'Yuri Pasholok's Journal' – http://yuripasholok.livejournal.com/

INDEX

References to images are in **bold**.